BREAKING

the

HUSH

FACTOR

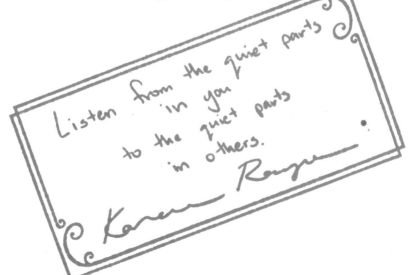

Listen from the quiet parts in you to the quiet parts in others.

Karen Rangen

Published by
Impetus Books
Austin, TX
www.impetus.pw

Special discounts are available on quantity purchases by schools, corporations, associations, and others. Book also available as an E-book. For details, contact the publisher at the address above.

ISBN 978-0-9897602-2-5
Cover design, layout design, and all illustrations
by Sam Killermann

Published June 2015
2 4 6 8 10 9 7 5 3

I dedicate this book to the people I love and the people who love me. I am lucky to have so many of you.

I also dedicate this book to all my students, young and old. You have taught me so much!

There are a few people in my life who deserve special attention:

Robert Heil, my funny and brilliant co-parent

Julia and Arwyn, my funny and brilliant daughters

Sam Killermann, my funny and brilliant publisher and friend

The four of you have shown extraordinary patience and care. Thank you.

TABLE OF
Contents

Heather Corinna

Founder & Director of Scarleteen

Karen Rayne is a sexuality educator and advocate with a rare gift: she has always appeared equally, and greatly, skilled at educating and advocating for youth and parents alike. Few of us can make that claim, but if she wanted to, she truly could.

If you're a parent or guardian, she's got your back. The same would be just as true if you were a young person. That, all by itself, makes her such a wonderful person, with such perfect perspectives, to write something like this, because that real balance is so essential to help people to start doing this truly well by everyone involved: all of a family, not just some.

What you've got in your hands here is qualified, caring help from one of the best and brightest sexuality and family educators in our field; one who really gets what young people want and need, and who has a great deal of love and respect for them. I know she can do an amazing job of helping you to do your best by young people in this area where they're done by so poorly with such unfortunate frequency.

Karen also knows that what you don't know, or feel intimidated or lost in, isn't something you need feel any shame about. Like so much of parenting, it's just something to work through and work to always get better and better at, while, hopefully, being kind to and forgiving of yourself. She knows that, and that compassion, understanding and gentle acceptance rings through all of this book. I predict you'll be pleasantly surprised to find how comforted and supported she can make you feel while learning about things so many people feel so uncomfortable and so unsupported with. She believes and trusts you want to do this well, and has every confidence that you can. If anything has kept you from these conversations so far, or from having them be beneficial and constructive, she's not going to make you feel bad about it, or suggest you're not a good parent. She knows even the best parents aren't magically experts at everything, or automatically sexually enlightened just by virtue of having become parents. She gets and recognizes that parents are people: nothing more but also nothing less.

I've dedicated most of my time and energy in the last two decades to working directly with young adults and their sexualities. I have a good sense of what's often missing at home for many of them, and of what could usually be improved. During that time, I've found few resources I feel excited to suggest to parents. For the most part, if something has the kind of respect, sensitivity and candor I think is so vital about adolescents, their families, and human sexuality, it often lacks the practical how-to. If something has the practical how-to, it often talks about young people, their families or sexuality in flawed or even deeply problematic ways. It's clear to me that the authors of some parenting guides have primarily, or even solely, engaged with parents, and only rarely, selectively, or very shallowly with adolescents. The material that actually does cover all of those bases, then often turns out only to address and acknowledge families made up of people who are only heterosexual, gender-conforming, or otherwise held up as culturally "normal" people. If you've looked for the kind of material and approaches that I have, this dearth of solid resources is probably sadly familiar to you, too.

That's why I'm so happy that Karen has created this guide. It ticks the boxes I want it to: all the boxes I know are essential to really help families — everyone in them — with this, and to actually feel like help, like real support. It's both clear and concise, while still giving so much depth. There is more out there than just this book, but not a lot. And from my reading, and also based on what I know about Karen as a person, educator and advocate, I just feel that you couldn't be in better hands. She's someone, and this book is something, that can tangibly help you not only do all of this better, but can help you knock this completely out of the park.

The information here isn't just guidance about parenting well when it comes to sex and sexuality. It's solid guidance about how to be a better parent — or other supportive adult — period. So much of what is in here is the panacea to many of the struggles and frustrations young people often experience with and express about parents and other adults; what leaves them feeling unheard or unseen, left adrift and unsupported instead of heard, seen, engaged and supported at a time in life when we know they often need and want just as much of all that (albeit in different ways) as they did in infancy and early childhood.

I hope you enjoy and appreciate it as much as I have, and have no doubt that you will.

Heather Corinna
Founder and Director, *Scarleteen.com*
Author, *S.E.X.: The All-You-Need-to-Know-Progressive Sexuality Guide to Get You Through High School and College*
April 26, 2015

P.S. There's an extra bonus for you in this book, and more to the point, in the things it invites you to think about and do, that is of big potential benefit to you, all by yourself, and your own sexuality, for yourself. Doing the kind of work around yourself, your own sexuality, your sexual history and current sexual life, and your thoughts and feelings about all of it, and using the new thoughts and feelings that tend to get triggered when parenting adolescents for your own positive growth, is very likely to personally benefit you, and improve your own sexuality, sexual life and your other intimate relationships outside the one you have with your children. And even that isn't entirely selfish, because it has legs: when you're more at home and at peace with sexuality for yourself, it's a lot easier, and more rewarding, to parent well around this issue and to help the young people that are part of your family to feel at ease with their own sexualities.

Some Introductions Don't Matter, but This One Really, Really Does.

And I'm not just saying that because I'm the author.

Because you've picked up this book, on some level you are ready to start talking about sex with your teenager. Or at least you're ready to start thinking about talking about it! I'm not going to spend a lot of time here covering why talking about sex with your teen is important—mostly because I assume you already have a sense of that importance, or else you wouldn't have picked up this book. But lest you forget, let me assure you: talking with parents about sex and sexuality has far-reaching influences on teens' sexual decision making and their sexual activities. This is true regardless of race, religion, sexual orientation, socioeconomic status, country of origin, or any of the many other ways that we divide and categorize humans.

And what makes the biggest difference is that those conversations are held in such a way that the teen feels her parent is a loving, supportive presence (I'm using "she" and "he" alternately in each chapter—more on that later). For that reason, this book is primarily a "how" book rather than a "what" book. Regardless of your individual perspective—political, religious, or otherwise—I hope that this book will give you more tools to talk with and listen to your teenager.

Each time your child or teenager comes to talk with you about something important or interesting in her life, you are auditioning for a chance to have another conversation down the road. This might sound and feel high stakes, which is not my intention. Rather, I want to make you aware that each conversation is valuable and important—if not in the immediate moment, then in the role it plays for future conversations and long-term goals.

YOUR LONG-TERM GOAL

The end goal of all education and conversations about sexuality, dating, romance, sexual orientation, gender, and more with teenagers is this: **physically and emotionally healthy adult sexuality**. This can be a scary goal for some parents to fully admit, but I hope you see the wisdom and the logic in it. Education in general is not designed to be used in the immediate moment—it is designed to be of lifelong use. First graders don't learn math because they need to solve a quadratic equation. They begin to develop the basic competencies that will serve them throughout life, whether that's knowing the correct change they are supposed to receive in a financial transaction, or filing a tax return. Likewise, learning about sexuality as a teenager doesn't mean we as parents need to queue the porn music. We are helping them develop the core competencies that will serve a lifetime of decision making. The end goal of physically and emotionally healthy adult sexuality is going to be a key point in everything you do moving forward.

In order to break this idea down a little bit, we need to start with this idea of physically and emotionally healthy adult sexuality. This goal really is long term: it's about providing an emotion- and knowledge-based sexual scaffolding for teens that they can draw on as adults when they are faced with decisions or questions. These skills are needed after high school and for the rest of a person's life. Making sexually smart decisions is not only something that is necessary prior to marriage, but is also an integral part of a committed relationship.

Emotional sexual health is about emotional intelligence, both in and out of sexual and romantic relationships. It offers knowledge of oneself and the ability to communicate clearly with a current or potential partner. It is also about self-compassion, self-esteem, and self-acceptance. Being healthy in all of these ways results in an adult who is self-composed and able to make sexual decisions out of a deep understanding of self and what is best for oneself and for one's partner.

Physical sexual health involves the obvious: a reduction of unplanned pregnancies and infections, but also general knowledge about issues like cancers, general reproductive health, and how and when to test for STIs (sexually transmitted infections, also known as sexually transmitted diseases or STDs).

While these hallmarks of emotional and physical sexual health are important regardless of age, assumptions that parents and other adults make about when it is appropriate for a young person to become sexually active can stymie the sexuality education they provide to a teenager.

WHAT IS AGE-APPROPRIATE SEX ED, ANYWAY?

Everyone agrees that "age-appropriate" sex ed is definitely the way to go. None of us wants to be either too far behind or too far ahead of our children and teens. It's a little like *Gol*ilocks an* the Three Bears*, except that instead of a mouth burn, we think we are at risk of "ruining everything" if we don't get it "just right."

Let's start by taking the potential horror stories down a notch. Yes, it would be really nice if we could address a sexual topic with our children or teenagers about two days before

Goldilocks and the Three Outcomes of Sex Ed

Too Hot.   Just right.   This kid is ruined.
                                       Pack it up. Make
                                       a new one.

they needed the information. That way, they would have a little time to think through what we had talked about, we could follow up, and they would be ready at just the right moment.

But that's not possible. Instead, we have to make some "best guesses"—and those best guesses have to be made based not only on your child, but on your child's culture, social background, and, most importantly, your child's peers. If your child's peer group is talking about sex, your child needs to be having conversations with you about the same things. I wish this could be easier, but it's not. There's no magic "age-appropriate" group of topics that work for all children, in all neighborhoods, across all of human culture.

Here are some basic pieces of information to help inform your decision about what might be "age-appropriate" for your children, in your family, and influenced by their peers:

- Most children have had a conversation about sex with a peer by age eight.
- Most children have viewed porn by age fourteen.[1]

---

1 M. A. H. Horvath et al., "Basically...porn is everywhere: A rapid evidence as-sessment on the effects that access and exposure to pornography has on children and young

- Most children do not ask their parents about the information they get from their peers or pornography.
- There is a set of high-quality National Sexuality Education Standards; you can find them and read them online at: http://www.FutureOfSexEd.org/fose-standards.html.

But don't just take this information and run with it. Averages and best practices are not the same thing as your individual child. Are your child's friends mostly highly media-savvy, pop culture-engaged youth? If they are, your kids will probably need information a year or two earlier than average.

The best way to figure this out is to ask the teachers and parents of older children in your child's school: When do kids usually start talking about _____? When do kids usually start experiencing or engaging in _____? (Where you can fill in the blank with kissing, intercourse, pornography, birth control, sexual harassment, and/or many other things.) Ask as many adults involved in your child's social circles as possible and take an average of those ages. Then, go a step further and get to know your teen and her friends—joke around with them, go to movies with them, eat dinner with them. Spend as much time as you can quietly driving, cooking, cleaning, or reading while your child has those friends over. Listen to what they say without interfering. What is actually age-appropriate sexuality education has much more to do with the actual young person in front of you and much less to do with theory.

Moving beyond what is immediately relevant at a given age is part of the movement toward your ultimate goal: physically and emotionally healthy adult sexuality. Thinking about this education as something you're providing for a lifetime of healthy adult sexuality can ease some of the discomfort around finding exactly the "right" time to have a given conversation.

WHAT YOUR LONG-TERM GOAL MEANS ABOUT THE ADOLESCENT YEARS

Keeping the long-term goal of healthy adult sexuality in mind can inform immediate interactions in important ways. Parents need to stay connected with their teens, so they can enter into conversations with them in appropriate ways.

It can be scary to acknowledge that your teenager is quickly becoming an adult, outside of the protected realm of your home. The fact is that your work as a hands-on parent is quickly coming to an end. While you've never been able to keep your child safe in every way from everything, you have had a large amount of control. But your role is shifting.

Here is an analogy that a friend recently told me that I think expresses the situation quite well: When you have a baby and a child, you are that little person's manager. When your child becomes a teenager, you are fired outright from your job as manager, and you have to work your butt off trying to be hired back on as a consultant. As a consultant, you have to accept that your teenager might make decisions that are different from the decisions you would make.

Nevertheless, your teenager can probably give a good approximation of the decision you would want her to make in a given situation. Your teen has spent her lifetime figuring you out. There's generally not much need to continue to defend your position by restating it. That's going overboard. Rather, your new, emerging job is to provide unconditional support and love. I know, I know—you say you've always done that. But now you have to do it while allowing your teen to make her own choices—and that can be really difficult.

An internal shift of your theoretical understanding of your role relating to your teenager, whether it's that of auditioning for future conversations or acting as a consultant

rather than a manager, will likely be helpful to you. It allows you to approach your teen in a way she will appreciate and respond to, and then she'll come back later for more conversations with you. This book will help you make that cognitive shift.

WHAT THIS BOOK IS AND WHAT IT IS NOT

This book serves as a guide for how to talk with your teenagers about sex, sexuality, and relationships. It is not just about passing on the specifics of biology and reproduction but refers to the much wider range of material that must be thought about and weighed during adolescence.

This book is also not intended to be a list of material to be covered; it is not a curriculum. There are too many eventualities that can arise during adolescence for me to provide you with a useful or encompassing way to respond in every situation.

Instead, this book provides a compass, an approach to

communication, that will open doors and smooth some of the rocks from the dirt path of communication between you and your teen.

The ten rules presented in this book to approaching the tricky subject of sex will let you jump into the new game of supporting your teenager to make her own choices. Supporting your teen's decisions will ultimately allow you more influence in her life, not less. While you may be disappointed in your limited role as a supporting character in this game, accepting this role and working with it will ultimately hold far more benefits for you, your teenager, and your relationship.

Regardless of your personal leanings (and this point is critical to all of your upcoming conversations with your teen), "sex" is more than just intercourse. "Sex" in this book encompasses sexuality, and romance, and dating, and much more—and so should you in your conversations with your teenager. Chapter 9 includes a list of topics that should be covered in sexuality education. If you think your teenager is getting high-quality sexuality education outside your home, look at the topics covered. Are most of the topics on the list in this book covered in the curriculum? If not, your teenager isn't getting all of the information she needs, and you're going to need to supplement at home or bring in a third party to either work with her individually or work with a group of teenagers, including your teen. However, if your teenager is getting a full sexuality education outside of the home, the conversations that you will hold can focus on her experiences, physical and emotional, rather than more broadly discussed facts and theories of sexuality.

My goal with this book is to show you how to have good conversations about sexuality with your teenager and to encourage you to gather your courage and have those conversations. I hope that after reading and implementing these rules over time, you will feel comfortable and at ease in conversations with your teenager about sexuality and romance. However, the conversational skills and guidelines presented here need not be restricted to only the topic of sexuality. They can apply to any topic about which you're having a hard time relating with your teenager: drugs, school, home, family, friends, everything!

WHO THIS BOOK IS FOR

This book is designed for parents and those in a parenting role. It is intended for every adult who engages with teenagers in such a way that the subject of sex and sexuality may come up. I have written the book for and addressed to parents because parents often find themselves without training, experience, or support in talking with their teenagers about sex and sexuality. But I hope that this book will be used by a much wider range of people. I hope that aunts, uncles, teachers, ministers, volunteers, and many others will find my guidance useful.

The parental role is a little different from other adult roles. Teenagers can respond differently to their parents than to other adults in their lives. This isn't surprising because parents have a uniquely important role in their children's lives. Parents have substantial impact over their child's life for a long time, but during adolescence the pendulum is beginning to swing (or has already swung) the other way. It can suddenly seem like the parent has no impact at all. It may seem like the parent has less influence over their teenager's sexual and romantic choices than anyone—and everyone!— else in the world. On the face of it, this may be the case. But on the inside, it's not. Parents hold enormous sway with their teenagers—and so do many other adults.

Because I suspect that most readers of this book will be

parents, that's how I address the reader. But if you fill another role with the teen(s) in your life, please mentally substitute your role every time you read the word "parent."

This book can be used by parents of adolescents across the gender identity and sexual orientation spectrum. The worries, triggers, and content of conversations with teens who identify as transgender, gay, lesbian, bisexual, queer, or one of the other myriad ways that human sexuality expresses itself may be different, but the approach to the conversations is just the same.

This book is not meant to support families who are grappling with crippling emotional or sexual issues. If your teen has substantial emotional issues, has been abused, or is becoming physically or emotionally abusive of you, you will need to seek help elsewhere. (This book might augment that support, but it is by no means sufficient to replace that support.) In these cases, I recommend finding a therapist to support you through this process.

This book is also not designed to be enough support for parents whose teenagers are in emotionally or physically abusive relationships. Abusive adolescent relationships are regrettably common and require an additional level of intervention and support, for both the parent and the teen, that is beyond the capacity of this or any other book. For information on how to recognize and respond to relational abuse, you can call your local women's shelter or you can visit the resources page on my website at www.HushFactor.com/resources.

THE TEN RULES

Each of the ten chapters in this book is based on one of the ten rules that lead to higher quality, more engaging conversations between parents and their teens. They are or-

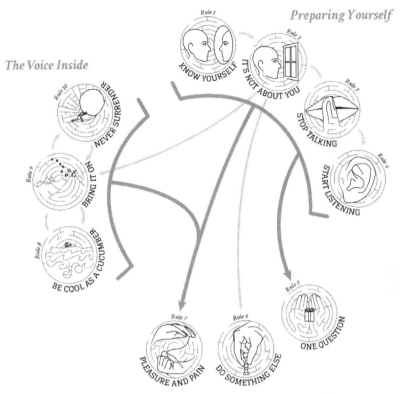

ganized into three sections. The first section highlights the parent's transition, starting with their internal perspective of themself and their contribution to the conversation. The middle of the book focuses on parents' explicit interactions with their teen during conversations. The final portion provides needed support to continue the conversations in the long term. In brief:

Ten Rules for Talking with Teens about Sex

1   **Know yourself.** What are your expectations, your hopes, and your fears about your teenager's sexual and romantic development? You will have far more control over yourself and your interactions if you have a full

understanding of these things.

2. **Remember that it's not about you.** Your teenager is discovering sex and sexuality for the first time. She wants to talk about her current exciting, overwhelming path. Let her! That's how you'll find out what you can do to help your teenager walk this path—and that's what matters most.

3. **Stop talking!** As the parent of a teenager, you are in the business of getting to know your teenager, not giving information to your teenager, or telling her what to do. If you're talking, you can't hear what your teenager is trying to tell you about herself.

4. **Start listening!** Stop talking. Start listening. Your primary role as a parent is to learn about your teenager's evolving self. That can't happen if you don't really, really listen.

5. **You only get one question.** Since there's only one, you'd better make it a good one that can't be answered with a yes or a no. Spend some time mulling it over. You can ask it when you're sure it's a good one.

6. **Do something—anything!—else.** Find something to do while you're talking. Many teenagers will have an easier time talking about sexuality and romance if you're doing something "side by side" like driving, walking, or playing a game rather than sitting and looking at each other.

7. **About pleasure and pain.** You have to talk about both. If you don't acknowledge the physical and emotional pleasure associated with sexuality in addition to the pain, your teenager will think you're completely

out of touch and won't talk with you. Then you will actually be completely out of touch.

8 **Be cool as a cucumber.** It is only when you manage to have a calm, loving demeanor that your teenager will feel comfortable talking with you. And remember, you're in the business of getting to know your teenager, and the only way to do that is if your teenager keeps talking.

9 **Bring it on!** Your teenager has tough things she wants to talk about, and some of them might even be specific and technical. If you're able to engage in these conversations with honesty, humor, and no judgment, your teenager will feel much more at home coming to you with the increasingly difficult emotional questions that touch her heart.

10 **Never surrender.** There may be times you feel like quitting. Like the millionth time when you've tried to have an actual conversation with your teenager (about anything, much less sex!) and your teenager has once again completely avoided eye contact and has not even acknowledged your existence. But you can't. You have to stay engaged. You're still building your long-term relationship. Keep going. Trust me.

While the rules are (necessarily) presented in this linear fashion in the book, that doesn't mean that they are inherently linear in nature. There are interactions between these rules that are important to a full understanding and execution of them. I have a complex-looking diagram of how the ten rules interact and mutually support each other. One of the basic tenets of the diagram is that the ten rules are broken up into three areas of focus. I will introduce these sections in more depth later, but here is a brief overview now.

The first section of this book, Preparing Yourself, covers the first four rules. This addresses how you, as a parent, need to prepare yourself to dive into the coming conversations with your teenager. The second section of this book, When You and Your Teen Talk, covers the next three rules. This section of the book addresses a few details of your linguistic and physical interactions with your teen during conversations. The last section of the book, The Voice Inside, comprises the last three chapters. This last section serves as a support for both your internal state during conversations and encouragement for you to continue having those conversations.

You can take a look at the graphic now, if you want to, but don't take the details to heart quite yet. I will go into the graphic and the interacting details involved in the last chapter.

ON MY USE OF GENDER PRONOUNS, EPIGRAPHS, AND WORKBOOK SPACES

An ongoing challenge for authors is the linguistic choice of gender pronouns for a person of unspecified or generalizable gender identity. Because the ten rules here are designed for both adults and teens of all gender identities, I yearn for the gender-neutral singular pronoun that the English language lacks. Some authors choose to use the plural "they, theirs, them" as a substitute for a gender-neutral singular, but I find that approach awkward. Instead, I alternate between "she, her, hers" and "he, him, his" between chapters. In this introduction, I've begun with the female pronoun and I continue from there. But none of the content in this book is gender specific; it is inclusive of everyone. You know the genders of your children, so make the appropriate mental substitutions as you read.

At the beginning of each chapter, you will find an epigraph: a few words to introduce the theme. I've written all but one of these, with the goal of offering you a unique way to consider the primary goal of that chapter, with a more lyrical, poetic form. You can use these as a mind-set to begin the chapter or as a meditative focus to process the chapter.

Also scattered throughout this book are little spaces with invitations and suggestions for you to think and write on the topic at hand. These can be used in a number of ways. You can use them as they're presented: read the prompt, write your response. You can also use them as conversation starters with a co-parent, questions to ponder while you're driving to work, or even things to bring up with your teen directly. Regardless of how you use the workbook spaces, I hope you will see this book as a living, interactive experience. Write your thoughts in the margins as they come up—or if you're reading the e-book version, have a pad of paper and a pen next to you or an open document on your digital device. Interactive consideration of your parenting life is an integral part of the rules. You will get much more out of the experience if you engage with it, in whatever way you feel most comfortable.

And now, on to section 1! (And don't you feel better prepared to begin section 1 now that you've read the introduction?)

Preparing Yourself

As you begin your journey toward open dialogue with your teen about sex and sexuality, you need to first turn your gaze inward. If the dialogue begins before you have a clear understanding of self, you may respond without thinking about what you really mean and what you really want to say. This section asks you to consider your own perspectives of what adolescent sexuality is, could be, and should be—and how your teen is in reference to all of those things.

The four chapters in this section are:

1. Know Yourself
2. It's Not about You
3. Stop Talking
4. Start Listening

If you take a peek at the diagram of the ten rules on page 11, you'll notice that everything flows from these first four rules. These are the bedrock rules of your conversations with your teen. While it may seem appealing, and perhaps even prudent, time-wise, to jump directly to section 2, which covers your actual interactions with your teen, I hope that you won't. This section is the metaphorical stretching before the running in your family conversations about sexuality.

Know Yourself

The center of a circle is its balance point.
The balance of my relationships is at my center.
I will find my center in order to begin.

When it comes to communicating with your teenager about sexuality, you must start by knowing yourself. You have expectations, hopes, and fears about your teenager's sexuality and romantic explorations. Every parent does. To have good conversations about sexuality and romance with your teenager, you must be clear with yourself about your own perspectives before you start. Take some time to get to know yourself, internally clarifying how you really feel and what you really hope for your teen's sexuality at his current stage of development and how he will move forward into adulthood. This understanding will form the basis of your ability to have productive conversations with your teenager, so take your time. Relish getting to know and understand these parts of yourself.

YOUR EXPECTATIONS

Clarifying your expectations means articulating what you expect your teenager will do on his path to adult sexuality. You may or may not actually want your child to do these things, but you think they will happen. Here are some examples:

"I expect my teen to say what he wants romantically and sexually."

"I expect my teen to keep his romantic and sexual engagements to himself, both at home and at school."

"I expect my teen will not be sexually or romantically interested in anyone until he's in high school."

"I expect my teen will try to have sex with girls."

"I expect my teen to have sex soon."

There are many more expectations that you might have! It's important to know what those expectations are, because they affect how you communicate with your child. Here's an example: Susan has a young teenage son, Alfred. Susan did not date or have sex until her twenties, and she expected the same from Alfred. But this expectation was subconscious. It took time and introspection before Susan was able to state this expectation clearly. We'll come back to Susan's and Alfred's story in a minute. Before you read on, take some time to figure out how you expect your teenager to engage (or not engage) sexually and romantically over the course of his teenage years.

Expectations about your teen's sexual and romantic life generally come from three places: (1) your own personal romantic and sexual experiences as a teenager, (2) statistics and trends in current adolescent sexual activity, and (3) careful assessment of your own teen. Your personal experiences and general societal trends are both relatively helpful ways to start thinking about adolescent sexuality in general terms. But they have very little to offer in terms of what specific experiences your teenager will have or the choices he will make. The problem is that your personal experiences are too limited in scope while trends and statistics are too wide in scope.

When parents expect their teenager's potential activities to mirror their own adolescent choices and experiences, the parents are forgetting that their teen has had unique experiences growing up and has become a particular individual person.

Going back to Susan and Alfred, Susan expected Alfred to be relatively uninterested in sex and romance through his teens, "because that's how we do things in our family." Susan made broad assumptions about her son without taking his personal developmental trajectory into account. When Su-

Workbook
Expectations for Your Teen

I expect my teen to feel...

I expect my teen to do...

I expect my teen to love...

21

san vocalized her assumption and her reasoning behind it, she realized its inappropriateness and was able to move past her expectations to look more clearly at her son as an individual growing up in a very different context than she had grown up in.

On the other end of the spectrum of misappropriated assumptions are societal trends. When parents expect their teenager's potential activities to be smack-dab in the middle of the average statistical bell curve, they are forgetting that there's a tail on both sides and someone has to end up there, too. Statistics are useful for a principal who runs a school of six hundred students. Statistics are not useful for a parent who is trying to connect with an individual teenager. However, the larger problem is not actually statistics, but the over-the-top rumors that occasionally sweep the country about teenagers' sex lives. I am continually called upon to refute misconceptions that the majority of teenagers are suddenly engaging in group sex, wearing different color bracelets that indicate what sexual activities they are on the prowl for, or are taking illegal hormones to look more like the other sex. There are probably teenagers doing all of these things across our large and varied country, but none of these trends are sweeping the nation in large numbers. Just because you've heard that "all teenagers" are doing one thing or another doesn't necessarily mean that your teenager is doing it. When you hear rumors or statistics that scare you, breathe deeply and refocus your attention on your teen, the one and only teenager you need to be really thoughtful about right now. While it is sometimes useful to take rumors like this and use them as discussion points with your teenager, it's important to discuss it in the context of a few people choosing to do something rather than a fad that is sweeping middle or high schools across the country.

It is through attending to the personality, choices, and

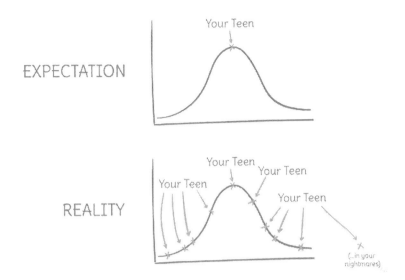

quirks that make up your specific teenager that you will find the clearest and most appropriate expectations. This is hard to do!

Subconsciously falling back on your experiences, general rumors, and statistics as a way to form expectations for your teenagers' sexual choices can be harmful, and it might be hard to recognize that this is what you're doing, at first. Given time and conversation with your co-parents, your friends, your teenager's teachers, and most of all your teenager, you will be able to gain a clearer lens through which to view your teenager's potential romantic and sexual life.

This is not to say that you will be able to predict your teenager's choices. By seeing your teenager clearly, you may gain a general idea of his decision-making trajectory, but specific predictions are difficult if not impossible. There are three reasons why predicting your teenager's behavior is particularly difficult at this stage: (1) as teenagers are in a constant state of personal evolution, their sexual decision-making processes may evolve, too; (2) many teenagers hide parts of themselves from adults; and (3) often teenagers' most important decisions will be made when they are with their peer group rather than when they are with you. As a result, even a truly clear view of your teenager won't allow you to make accurate predictions of his future thoughts and behaviors. It is most helpful, therefore, to release any lingering expectations you might have, and move on to focus on your hopes and fears.

Hopes and fears are about what you want and fear for your teenager, but they are not actually about your teenager. They are actually about you. It is much more effective to claim your hopes and fears as your own rather than putting them on your teenager. Let's talk a bit about hopes, and then a bit about fears. These are heavy issues. Working through your own issues will provide you with a clear and open place from which to talk with your teenager about these very hard topics.

YOUR HOPES

Everyone has hopes about their teenagers' sexuality. These hopes can cover a wide range of topics, but generally they focus on the teenager making what the parent would consider to be wise decisions. Here are some examples of hopes that parents might have about sex and sexuality:

"I hope my teen loves the first person he has sex with."

"I hope the first person my teen has sex with loves him."

"I hope my teen graduates from high school a virgin."

"I hope my teen is a virgin when he gets married."

"I hope my teen really enjoys his sex life."

"I hope my teen is kind to the people he has sex with."

"I hope my teen knows I'm OK with it if he masturbates."

"I hope my teen knows how to use a condom correctly."

"I hope my teen has sex with several lovers so that he can come to know himself better sexually."

"I hope my teen is straight."

Being clear about what you hope for your teenager's sexuality will aid you dramatically as you move into conversation with him about sex and sexuality. What are your hopes for your teen's sexuality?

Take fifteen minutes and write them down. Be brutally honest with yourself. You don't need to share these hopes with your teenager or anyone else, but you do need to fully understand them yourself.

Sometimes parents are afraid to acknowledge their hopes about positive sexuality for their teenagers because they are worried that any statement of hope about sexuality will encourage intercourse. When you were pondering your hopes, did you express hopes for your teenager to be healthfully sexually active at some point in his life? Consider this potential hope parents may have for their teenager: **Physically and emotionally healthy adult sexuality**. What is your immediate reaction to this hope?

Remembering that there are positive ways for your teenager to both experience sexuality and ex-

Workbook

Hopes for Your Teen

I hope my teen will feel...

I hope my teen will do...

I hope my teen will love...

Immediate Reactions

My immediate reacton to "Pysically and emotionally healthy adult sexuality" is...

Sexuality is positive for people in the following ways...

Workbook
The Source of Your Hopes

Write your hopes as a list and for each one identify the reason you have this hope for your teenager and what you think might be its original source.

press sexuality is good for you and good for your relationship with your teenager. Rather than regarding conversations about sexuality to be about stopping all forms of sexual expression by your teenager, these conversations are really about supporting your teenager in a deeper understanding of healthy sexual expression. This book will focus on physically and emotionally healthy adult sexuality as the primary goal for your conversations with your teenager about sex and sexuality.

Now that you have your hopes written out, it is time to start thinking about why you hope for those things. Some parents have hopes for their teenager's sexuality based on their own past choices, either choices they felt well served by or choices they now regret. Other parental hopes are based on religious or moral beliefs. I include moral beliefs here because the reason behind the hope is not always strictly religious but can be more of a general sense of what is right and what is wrong. Sometimes parents' hopes are based in fear. Whatever the reason behind your hopes for your teenager's sexuality, it is important to realize what those rea-

Parental Well Wishing

"I'm going to need more coins."

sons are.

In addition to the reasons behind your hopes, it is helpful to consider the origins of your hopes. Are your hopes something that came to you because of your experiences, your religious background, what your parents wanted for you, or something entirely different? By recognizing the source of your hopes, you can evaluate their importance.

Take some time, as much time as you need, and figure out the reasons and then the sources for each of your hopes. Remember, this is a time and a place to be honest with yourself. Even if your reasoning is not logical or is not something you would be proud to admit, it is critical that you acknowledge the background for your hopes.

Continuing with our example mother and son pair from the earlier section, Susan began with the assumption that what was good for her sexually and romantically as a teenager and young adult would also be good for Alfred. She was using a variation of The Golden Rule: "Treat others as you want to be treated." I would like to propose that instead of following The Golden Rule with your teenagers, that you consider The

Platinum Rule, which was developed by Milton Bennett. The Platinum Rule says: "Treat others as they want to be treated." In Susan's case, this means being guided in how to proceed by considering Alfred as a person, rather than only considering her own personal history.

When Susan confronted her unspoken expectation that Alfred would be uninterested in sex and romance until his twenties, that he would benefit from the same things that she had benefited from, she was able to reframe her expectation as a hope. Susan came to see that what she was really hoping for was not this specific experience of waiting for sex and romance, but rather for age-appropriate, life-affirming sexual and romantic experiences according to Alfred's developmental trajectory. Because Susan's personal experience had been good for her, she had not considered the possibility that Alfred could have very different experiences that could be just as positive for him. Our conversation allowed Susan to again reframe her hope in more general terms that were open to and supportive of Alfred's personal and individual path. It is generally true that the reasons for parents' hopes are broader

The Golden Rule Says...

Susan should treat Alfred how she wanted to be treated as a teen.

MEET SUSAN
- Not interested in sex & romance as a teen
- Didn't date.
- Didn't want to.

MEET ALFRED
- Not Susan.

The Platinum Rule Says...

Susan should treat Alfred how he wants to be treated.

than the specific hopes. How does it feel to think about stepping back to those larger hopes rather than sticking with the more specific ones?

You may be experiencing a deeper understanding of yourself and how you expect and hope your teenager will act romantically and sexually. This process is focused on helping you increase your self-knowledge, which will in turn allow you to create an open conversation space between you and your teenager where more effective dialogue can happen. This open space will allow you to talk with your teenager about sexuality and romance without shutting him down. It can be hard work, but it will pay high dividends in the end by supporting the goal of your teenager having a healthy adult sexuality.

Hold on to the ideal of this open space between the two of you, because now it is time for you to consider the thing that can be the most intrusive to that open conversation space: Your fears.

YOUR FEARS

You know your expectations and your hopes. Now turn to your fears. Parents generally do have hopes about their teenager's sexuality, but they often have far more fears. Here are some examples of parental fears about their teenager's sexuality:

"I'm afraid my teen will get pregnant."

"I'm afraid my teen will get someone pregnant."

"I'm afraid my teen will get an STD/STI. Especially AIDS."

"I'm afraid my teen will have sex with many people."

"I'm afraid my teen will get hurt."

"I'm afraid my teen will be gay."

"I'm afraid my teen will hurt someone else."

"I'm afraid my teen will be raped."

"I'm afraid my teen will ruin his life."

"I'm afraid my teen will not listen to or believe what I tell him about sex."

"I'm afraid my teen will fall in love with someone who is just using him."

Making this list might take some time. Or it might all come out in one loud, long, exhausting sitting. Give yourself some space and let it happen in whatever way works best for you. But get out absolutely everything. In my classes, I find that parents often hold back that one last, most important fear. They don't want to say it, because saying it will acknowledge that it might happen. The same is often true for my younger students—they don't bring out their biggest, scariest questions or thoughts until the very end. Hiding from the big issues is a natural response—they're scary! But in the end, it doesn't serve anyone. While inherently scary, dealing with your big fears up front can allow you to tend to those fears and set them aside more quickly, giving you more time to have good conversations with your teenager. You don't have to show your list to anyone else. All you have to do is look at it and acknowledge your fears to yourself. Get everything out there, and remember that no worry or concern is too small or too big.

More often than not, it is parental fears that drive parents' conversations about sexuality with their teenager. Understanding your fears is the first step to taking control of your conversations, or rather the first step to releasing control of those conversations to your teenager. Handing over this control is what will allow the conversations to happen in really meaningful ways. With your teenager in control of the conversations, you will be able to focus on the issues that really matter, rather than the issues that are distracting you. Acting and speaking out of fear of what might happen in your teenager's life will not create a space where your teen feels comfortable talking with you. It is likely that your teen already has enough angst and fear over his sex life because it is new, big, exciting, terrifying, and many other highly emotional things. Your teenager has plenty to sort through without your issues getting tangled up in there, too. Now the work is on releasing, or at least addressing, your fears.

Here is a two-step process to work through each of the fears you wrote down, one by one:

1. Brainstorm at least two ideas (more is better!) on how your teenager's decisions could prevent or reduce the possibility of each fear. Don't just think of the "best" way, because this is restricting. As the saying goes, there are more ways than one to skin a cat. Similarly, there are many paths to healthy sexuality.

2. Brainstorm at least one way you could respond to each fear, were it to actually happen, that could be supportive of a healthy relationship between you and your teenager.

There are many possibilities for each of these brain-storming ideas. If you're having trouble, put your list down for a day or two and then come back to it. You can also use your social network—ask friends and family for their ideas. If you are really not able to think of any supportive people in your life, pop over to my website. I have a list of common fears and supportive responses—and a place to add new ones! You'll find the list at www.HushFactor.com/FearResponses. I promise that supportive responses exist for each and every one of your greatest fears.

The goal of this process is for you to see that your pre-ferred prevention methods are not the only ones available to your teenager. Your teenager may surprise you with thought-fulness and care, with recklessness, or with indifference. But whatever he brings you, you have the option of responding in a way that improves the quality of your relationship with your teenager rather than degrading it.

At the end of one of my parenting classes, a mother who had been quite contentious and angry through most of the class raised her hand and said she would like to say some-thing. I wasn't sure what to expect. She started crying and said, "What I have learned through this class is that my son will be OK even if he does have sex. Scary, bad things can happen. Pregnancies, STIs, heartbreak. These things and more might happen to my son. I certainly cannot ensure that they will not. But if they do, he will overcome them. And I will be by his side, cheering him on at every step." Every par-ent in the room started to tear up.

Parents have big, legitimate fears when their children start engaging romantically and sexually. But it is far more effective for you to speak and act out of hope and determina-tion that your teenager will reach the goal of physically and emotionally healthy adult sexuality than for you to speak and act out of unexamined expectations, hopes, or fears. Moving into this conversational space where you are open to your teenager, to truly supporting him without being tied to negativity, will allow your teen to trust you to listen and be supportive of his process and his life choices.

Your teenager does not embody your expectations, your hopes, or your fears. Your teenager is his own bird, and the beauty of his individual song and flight can only come when you allow him the space to be himself.

No, It's Not About You

Discovery is a beautiful thing.

Now that you've put attention toward getting to know yourself, it's time for you to release all of your remaining expectations, hopes, and fears about your teenager's sexual development. Your teenager is not the embodiment of these things, your teenager is her own person. Dealing with your own issues is critically important for you to be able to approach your teenager with that clear lens that allows you to focus on her. Release those expectations, hopes, and dreams! It's time to focus on your teenager.

You must always keep the focus of conversations about

sex and sexuality on your teenager or on generalities about sexuality (that is, those things that have nothing at all to do with your own sex life or the sex life you had as a teenager). Teenagers feel like they are discovering sex. And in very important ways, this is exactly what is happening—they are discovering their own sexuality. By talking about other people's sexual choices (yours, their older siblings', their friends', famous people's, whoever's), you are reminding them that they did not, in fact, invent sex; you are drawing their attention away from where it should be focused: on discovering themselves. This is not the time for you to do that.

I find that parents can get mired in the hope that their children will learn from their own (the parents') mistakes. This won't happen. It would be really, really nice if it could! What is more important for you, as a parent, is to pay attention to what lessons your teen is in the process of learning for herself, and to support that process in a thoughtful way.

To exemplify my point, here is an entirely nonsexual story for you that has deep implications for all parent-child conversations, but particularly conversations about sex and sexuality.

MARGARET AND THE FOREST

Once there was a young girl named Margaret. Margaret lived in a beautiful house on the edge of the suburbs with her father, her mother, and her little sister. One day when Margaret was nine years old, she decided to go exploring in the woods behind the house. This would be the first time for her to go into the woods alone.

Margaret ventured to the edge of her suburban lawn, craning her head this way and that way, trying to see through the trees without actually going into them. She imagined it would be cooler in there, under the shade. Margaret reached

out her hand and stretched it as far into the shade as she could. She admired the beautiful shadows of the trees on her skin and pretended that her fingertips indeed felt cooler than her shoulders, still out in the sun.

Margaret heard a beautiful birdcall from deep within the shadows, and she looked, trying to catch sight of this amazing bird that must be so much more colorful and interesting than any bird that flew over the sun-filled lawn. Suddenly something bright and fast darted between the trees, and Margaret was sure it was the same bird she had heard calling. She started to run after it, to see the colors more clearly, but she stopped a few feet into the forest. Now that she was all the way under the forest shade, it really was much cooler.

Under her feet, Margaret felt the leaves and the twigs crunching. Stooping down, she sifted through the debris and smelled something that was a bit like the compost pile in the corner of her own yard—but this was a much richer, much deeper, much older smell.

Margaret sat down. Then she lay down and closed her eyes. She stayed there, breathing in the smells and feeling

What is one long-term benefit and one short-term benefit Margret could have gained from the experience of her mother listening rather than sharing?

Why might those experiences have been important or useful for Margaret?[1]

---

1 Some of my answers to this question are interspersed in the following pages—but I'd like you to consider your answers first!

the sun and shade move back and forth over her closed eyes.

After some time, Margaret walked back to her house. The afternoon sun felt harsh after the coolness of the forest. Inside, Margaret ran to her mother, excited to share what had happened.

"Mama, I went into the forest alone! I heard birds, and I think I even saw one!"

"Oh, that's wonderful, dear!" said her mother. "You know, when I was about your age, I went into the forest alone for the first time, too. Ah, it was nice to go into the cool forest for the first time. The bird that you heard was probably a Vermillion Flycatcher. They're hard to find, but one day when I was a little girl I fell down a hill and found their nest. I'll show you where the hill is—but you can't go down there because it's too steep, and you'll fall. You should also be careful if you sit or lie down on the ground, because there are snakes around. I found all of the different kinds of snakes when I was a girl, and so I can tell you about each of them, what they look like, and whether they're poisonous or not. Oh, and you should be careful and not eat the plants you find in the forest. I tried many them when I was a girl, and while some of them are very good, it can be hard to tell them apart from the ones that make you sick, and I don't want you getting sick. What else did you do in the forest?"

"Um, nothing." Margaret wandered up to her room, wondering why she had been so excited to tell her mother about her trip to the forest. Her mother had already seen and felt everything she had seen and felt, plus much more.

Margaret's mother had the best of intentions in telling Margaret about the forest. She wanted to make sure that Margaret was safe, that Margaret didn't make the same mistakes that she had. But she went about it in all the wrong ways. If she had listened to Margaret share her experience in the forest, she would have learned that her daughter only went a few steps in—that she was not running full tilt after a mysterious bird to fall down a hill. She also would have learned that her daughter had not even thought of eating anything in the forest. Instead, the mother shared her own story, running over Margaret's own experiences. This significantly reduces the likelihood that Margaret will share in the future, because what it says to Margaret is that her mother is more interested in herself than she is in Margaret. The mother in this story failed this audition and will need to work hard to obtain another one.

Now, Margaret's mother did have safety information that Margaret needed. Because she was beginning to venture into the forest, Margaret needed to know that she shouldn't lie down because of the snakes and shouldn't eat anything because it could be poisonous. These things are better learned through conversation than through experience. But both Margaret and her mother would have been better served

had the mother talked about these important points in the abstract rather than through personal stories, through questions rather than lectures, and after giving her full attention to Margaret's complete experiences. After listening to the entirety of Margaret's story, without sharing any information of her own but listening attentively to what Margaret had to share, it's possible her mother could have brought up some of these safety issues. It would have been better still for the mother to wait a day—two days—three days—maybe even more for some children and teenagers. This allows the information to sound like just what it is—information, not a rebuke or a scolding. It allows for the young person to be fully excited (and rightfully so!) about her own experiences. The emergence into independence—into venturing into new situations alone whether sexual or otherwise—marks a new sort of inner life for young people. Parents who start by acknowledging and respecting that new inner life as fully independent and separate are better able to build a special, trusting relationship with their teen. The teenager learns to trust her parent—and, not being run over with ideas, suggestions, thoughts, and so on, the teenager learns to listen to the things the parent says with more attention.

Back to our story: The mother could have waited a few days until a window of opportunity arose—for example, either as she and Margaret passed by the forest at some point or because snakes or berries came up in some other context. Given this opening, here are ways the mother could have presented forest safety information to Margaret:

"There are some snakes in the forest—all over the place—and they're pretty hard to spot. If you're lying on the ground, they'll slither right over you! Some of them are poisonous, so it's important to stay up off the ground in the forest."

"Did you know there are two kinds of red berries in the forest? One's really poisonous—ugh, nobody wants to get that kind of sick! The two kinds of berries are a little hard to tell apart though—they look exactly alike, just the leaves on the plant grow a bit differently."

This approach would have kept Margaret's discovery of the forest as something personal rather than turning it into a trip down memory lane for her mother. Also, had the mother listened to Margaret's description of her time in the forest, she would have known that Margaret needed the information about the snakes sooner, but could probably wait for the information about the berries until sometime later.

Margaret's mother also seemed to forget that she went into the forest by herself and, although she faced dangers, she survived, learned, and grew from the experience. To take that process away from Margaret is unfortunate. We cannot keep our children safe from every pain, physical or emotional. But more to the point, we should not. It is through both happiness and pain that humans learn, and our children need the full range of those experiences.

Let's move back to discussing conversations about sex and sexuality and see how allowing these conversations to

Workbook
Focusing on Your Teen

What are some ways you can remind yourself that conversations with your teenager need to stay focused on her experiences?

What is a question you can ask yourself internally as a check for whether a conversation with your teen is appropriately focused on her?

be fully about your teenager works to both your advantage and your teenager's advantage.

One of the important parts of the story about Margaret is that she came to her mother very early on in her exploration of the forest. This is the case with most young people, as well—but they typically come to their parents for a first conversation long before their parents are aware or thinking about issues of their children's attraction and sexuality. These first conversations may not even register in the parent's attention—much like Margaret's conversation about the forest did not really register for her mother as something of note. Because first conversations are key, it's a good idea to get into a habit of paying attention to what your child or teenager has to say, specifically getting into a habit of letting her take the conversational reins. Listening to her perspective and hearing the stories she wants to tell will allow you to make all of your conversations be about her and her experiences rather than making them about you.

It can be scary for some parents to enter into any kind of conversation about sex or sexuality with their children or teenagers. But engaging fully in these early conversations allows both you and them to become more accustomed to the process. If you are already past the age for early conversations, if you are already into the ages where your teenager is talking about the scarier topics, letting your teenager talk about them openly with you will perhaps be harder, but just as beneficial. It can help to remember your ultimate goal for her: physically and emotionally healthy adult sexuality. Engaging in a thoughtful, open way, where the focus of the conversation is on your teenager, will allow her to reach this goal more effectively because you will know where she is coming from and what sorts of support and information she needs.

One way you can most effectively help this process of self-discovery happen is by encouraging your teenager's story of discovery to be about herself and no one else—not you, not her friends and peers, not rumors or stories. Just about your teenager. Of course, you will likely talk about friends, peers, rumors, stories, movies, advertisements, news events, and more. You may even find your teenager asking about your experiences—if she does, feel free to talk briefly about them or not, depending on your comfort level. (It is OK to decline to talk about your sexual history with your child. Everyone has the right to decline to talk about their sexuality with any person who asks, including you and your teen. You can say something like, "That's a really personal question and not something I want to talk about. Let's talk about sexual experiences in general rather than my specific experiences.") Talking about all of these things, or rather letting your teenager talk about, weigh, and consider all of these things, will provide opportunity for personal insight in remarkable ways. However, the essence of these conversations will be your teenager pondering the issues and events aloud, and how she might react or feel if she were in that position. Ultimately, the conversation remains about her even when the topic is someone else.

There is a common joke about a young couple who are completely physically enamored with each other: "They think they invented sex! Ha-ha!" But this joke touches on an important point: they actually did invent sex. At least, they invented sex within the context of their relationship. That sexual relationship had never existed before; sex between those two people is a brand new experience. The same point applies to teenagers: each teenager feels like she is inventing sex for the first time, because each teenager *is* inventing sex for the first time, for herself. When used in an attempt to pass on a lesson, teenagers will often discount a personal story because it allows them to say something like, "Well, that's not me! No one knows me!" Contrastingly, information that is broadly based and broadly presented can be taken in and applied much more directly to a teenager's decision-making process. We need to respect young people's experiences as valid and individual—and this includes their experiences of sex, love, and relationships.

Stop Talking!

The known is inside you.
It is the other that is mysterious.

Most parents talk too much. Way, way, way too much. It would be hard for me to overstate how much too much most parents talk. Everyone knows this. At least, anyone who has ever seen Peanuts cartoons—remember how the adults' dialogue was always represented by the wah-wah-wah of a trombone? This is the impression that most teenagers have of most adults: that the adults are lecturing monologues with little or no interest in what the teenager has to say.

Parents know this. They tell me, "I'll sit down and say, 'Let's talk about safe sex.' And she just tries to leave!" And then they say, "I keep trying to talk to my teenager about safe sex. I can talk until my face is blue, but it never gets through to her!" This is not entirely true; the things you say do matter and do sink in, but there are better ways of talking with your teen if blank stares are your typical response. The problem is that most teenagers associate conversations with their parents as their parents talking until they are blue in the face. It's not fun being lectured, and your teenager probably already sits through hours of lectures in school. Experiencing the same at home is not going to move your teenager toward any goal—and certainly not physically and emotionally healthy adult sexuality.

The tendency of parents to talk until they go blue in the face is particularly problematic with regard to sex because (1) your teen needs your help with common mistakes and lapses in judgment, (2) the fallout from a mistake or lapse in judgment could be life threatening or at least dramatically life altering, (3) there are religious/moral/ethical choices involved, and (4) the parent has no real control over it. The importance of the first two points plus the terrifying realization (if not acceptance) of the last one can send logical, well-meaning, generally well-acting parents over the deep end when they're talking about sex. Parents can lose their sense of direction in this area, and often they fall back exclusively on their moral compass and try to hammer home the importance of one religious/moral/ethical choice: "Don't have sex!" Parents who do manage to move beyond the don't-have-sex paradigm often stay focused on safer sex, condom usage, and so forth. While these are critical topics, teenagers have much more that they want—and need—to talk about.

When I was thirteen, we had a family friend living with us for a time. She was wonderful in many ways, and I benefited from her presence in my home. But she did one thing that drove teenage me crazy. About once a day, she would say to me, "Don't have sex." She said it under her breath, in passing, as if she were sending me a subliminal message. We could be passing in the hallway, eating dinner, having a conversation, anything, and right in the middle, she would say, "Don't have sex." And then continue on with whatever was actually happening. And now, years later, I know why I was bothered by her subliminal message: she talked too much. I don't think we ever sat down and had a real conversation about sex. I don't think she ever asked me if I was interested in having sex or if I had any questions about sex. She just told me not to do it. The effect was that I discounted what she had to say. I ignored her because she was talking too much without bothering to listen to me. And because I knew her apparently immovable position on the idea of me having sex, I'm not sure I would have entered into an honest conversation with her about sex anyway.

When I point out that parents talk too much in general, and specifically talk too much about sex, parents generally grasp the problem quickly, but they have a harder time finding a solution. You should have a head start on the solution because of the title of this chapter. The solution is for you,

the parent, to stop talking. Yes, I mean that in conversations with your teenager about sexuality and romance, you should do almost no talking—as little as you can get away with.

There are generally three objections that parents have when I suggest that they should stop talking as much as they have in the past:

1. "But my teenager won't talk. If I don't talk, no one will say anything!"

2. "I want to make sure my teenager understands our family's moral stance on sexuality. How can I make sure of that without talking?"

3. "You say I should make sure my teenager knows a bunch of things about safe sex, STIs, and more! How can I teach all that if I'm not talking?"

These are all really good questions, and we're going to touch on each of them.

"But my teenager won't talk. If I don't talk, no one will say anything!"

When teenagers pull away, as they often do, it is very hard on parents. It's painful to have your child pull away from you, emotionally, verbally, or physically. The mistake that parents make is that they try and fill that widening space between them and their teenager—with emotions, with words, with physical proximity. However, what is most beneficial for the teenager and for the parent-teen relationship is to just allow there to be some space—emotionally, verbally, and physically. You need to stay in proximity, but allow your teenager to see that you respect his space when he backs up.

It is relatively easy to see how to do this physically. You can stay in another part of the house, you can knock before opening a closed door and then wait to be invited in, you can sit a little bit further away on the couch than you used to, and you can allow your teenager to decline a kiss and a hug (remembering that all people need to be allowed, and even taught, how to give or withhold consent for physical contact). And you can do all of these things while continuing to be in the house with your teenager, going into his room for one reason or another, sitting on the couch together, and seeing your teenager with his friends. In fact, your teenager will be much more likely to grant you some level of proximity if you allow there to be space between you when he takes a step back.

The same theory applies to emotional distance. However, it's far trickier to keep emotional distance while maintaining proximity. While harder, appropriate emotional proximity is even more critical than physical distance. Emotionally speaking, you need to maintain your openness while allowing your teenager to be closed. This is a scary position to be in, remaining open to someone who is closed. Nevertheless, this is how you can remain in emotional proximity to your teenager while still allowing him space. If you can, work toward a deep, open trust that your teenager really loves you, even if he doesn't always act like it. Your teenager will be comforted by your emotional openness and will be much more likely to maintain an internal connection to you, even if he is unable to show it by emotionally reaching out himself.

This is not easy, either in theory or in practice. The art of feeling joyful curiosity and love toward your teenager when it does not seem to be returned may, some days, even be impossible. I am suggesting this level of openness as a goal that on some days you will meet and on other days you will not. Just don't give up on it! (See the last chapter for encouragement in the face of apparent failure!)

Now that you've gotten a general picture of what I mean

by allowing distance while maintaining proximity, physically and emotionally, we're going to get down to business and talk about verbal distance and proximity. This is an area where parents often have a lot of difficulty and have the most work to do.

The first and most important point I want to make is this: silence is OK. If your teenager is not talking, it is OK for you to be silent as well.

This is not to say that angry silence, awkward silence, avoiding silence, or other heavy, emotional silences are inherently good. But if you and your teenager are simply being together and neither of you is talking, that is the very essence of giving verbal space while remaining in proximity.

How does this allow for conversations about sexuality? It proves that you can respect your teenager's spoken or unspoken request for silence. And then when your teenager seems chatty, or at least chattier than usual, you can ask your one question. (I'll get into that more in chapter 5—you can skip ahead if you want, but be sure to come back here!) In addition to your one question, there will be times and places where topics come up naturally. This might happen through media (songs, movies, TV shows, video or computer games), through friends' or families' lives, or any number of other kinds of events. Take advantage of these fortuitous events by not talking (counterintuitive though it may seem). Ask your one question (chapter 5 again), and then listen, really listen to what your teenager has to say. (We go into the details of how to listen in chapter 4.) Unless your teenager asks for your feedback or thoughts or input, you should listen without giving any of these.

You and your teenager will become much closer if you follow these rules and learn to allow for silence.

"I want to make sure my teenager understands our family's moral stance on sexuality. How can I make sure of that without talking?"

There are many, many things for a parent of a teenager to worry about. This is not one of them. Go ahead and just scratch it off your worry list! Your teenager very likely already knows how you feel about sex and sexuality. Children become masters of understanding their parents' nuances, and your teenager was no different as a younger child. Your teenager spent many years studying you, learning how you interpreted and responded to the world and all of the individuals in it. Relish the fact that your teenager can probably pinpoint your beliefs about sexuality. If your teenager is off, he probably assumes you hold a more conservative view than you actually do.

Teenagers are in the process of formulating their own budding beliefs. They are not continuing to focus deeply on interpreting and understanding their parents' beliefs. So reinforcing your beliefs to your teenager will not persuade him to agree with you. Rather, let your teenager think through and process his own thoughts and reactions with you as a listener. Processing and analyzing his own reactions is a critical part of coming to his own beliefs, and doing so with you as a listener (not a talker or a commenter!) will allow you to serve as a constant reminder of your belief structure (which he knows!). By remaining present and showing respect for your teenager's process, you will ensure that your teenager thoughtfully and thoroughly considers your beliefs far more effectively than if you were verbally reiterating those beliefs.

"You say I should make sure my teenager knows a bunch of things about safe sex, STIs, and more! How can I teach all that if I'm not talking?"

This is a really good question. And the answer is relatively short: you ask what they think and know about these various topics when they come up naturally, and you answer their questions. Once you are able to stop talking to your teenager and start listening closely, you will find that your teenager will open up and start to ask questions. These topics will come up naturally. Many of their questions will flow right into the topics they need to learn about—because they are curious! We'll go into more detail on how to answer these questions in chapter 9.

"OK, I GET YOUR POINT. I'M ON BOARD. NOW HOW DO I DO IT?"

I'm glad you asked! And here's my answer: you don't talk. It really is that simple—in theory, at least. In practice, "just don't talk" can be a very difficult plan to implement. The absence of action is a hard concept for people to get. We're always doing something, so it can be easier to replace talking with something else. This is where active, attentive listening (chapter 4), formulating your one question (chapter 5), and doing something else like playing games, hiking, and so on (chapter 6) all come in handy. Parents who have come to me for help with their conversations with their children and teenagers about sex and sexuality have told me that this one tip—not talking—is the one that often makes the biggest difference.

Return to the story about Margaret in chapter 2, and rewrite the dialogue here. What might the conversation have looked like had Margaret's mother not said very much?

How did the dialogue turn out? Was Margaret chatty? Did she taper off and not really say much anyway? Children and teenagers have different rhythms to their expressions and speech, and will react differently, particularly if their parent has just changed their own patterns of conversation and communication.

And now chalk up that last group of thoughts to either your hopes or your fears about how he will react. It's likely that you're being overly hopeful or overly doubtful. The only way to know for sure is to jump in and give it a try. Don't expect just one day to do the trick, either. Give it a few months. See what happens. It could be beautiful.

Start Listening!

Listen from the quiet parts in you
to the quiet parts in others.

Listening is different from hearing. You can hear what someone says without really listening in the same way that you can read a sentence or a paragraph and not really have paid any attention to the content. The difference, of course, is that when you're reading, you can just go back over the part you didn't focus on and reread it. It's annoying, but no harm done. When you have heard, but not really listened to your teenager, you have to ask her to repeat herself or try to catch up without her noticing. That can hurt her feelings, make her less likely to come to you in the future, and generally put a rift in your relationship.

Learning to listen in that way is something that can take years. But it's worth it. It enriches both your and your teenager's experiences and your shared relationship. Your relationship with your teenager has years and years to come after she is no longer a teenager—and it's worth putting in extra effort, time, and attention when she *is* a teenager so that, as she transitions into adulthood, your relationship is on stable ground.

Learning how to access a quiet, internal space is the first step in the slow process of listening really well. Finding it inside yourself is the first thing. It is not an actual, physical spot (although thinking about such a place might help trigger your access to it). It is more about a state of mind—an emotional state of mind. When you are alone and calm, that is the best moment to try to access your quiet, internal space. You might find that certain places, music, smells, activities, or other physical things will help you access that space. If you meditate, you might already be familiar with it.

This is the space where most people tuck away their most private feelings. Joys or pains, large or small, recent or long past, these feelings take up root here. Your quiet space may be complicated, messy, not necessarily a pleasant place to stay focused on. But it is also a space that gives you access to your own feelings and reactions, and to the underlying feelings and reactions of those around you. People who have access to this space often move a little more slowly, emotionally speaking. They are less likely to jump to a reaction because they are aware of the complexity of feelings and decisions. Try to find that emotional space inside yourself, where you are not inclined to react quickly, but rather to want to listen even more. Spend some time with yourself to see what it feels like to have that quiet, still center as your starting place. Your quiet internal space gives you a vantage point from which to listen—to invite the person you are talking with to keep sharing of herself. It is a space of learning and interest, not a space of reaction. Do this alone first, before you try to access your quiet space while you're talking with your teenager or anyone else.

Once you've found your quiet place, the next step is to try to stay there during a conversation. This may be best to try out with a friend rather than with your teenager. See how it feels to listen to a friend from this emotional space. Do you feel grounded, centered, and open? Are you focused on your friend rather than on your internal dialogue or your own emotional reactions? If you're not quite there yet, it's OK. Spend some more time thinking and writing about your quiet space and practicing with a friend. This continued practice doesn't mean you have to stop reading through these rules—learning to listen from a quiet space may take years. You can continue developing your listening skills, along with the other skills in this book, at the same time.

At some point, you'll move on to a conversation with your teen. The goal is for you to feel safe accessing what often feels like a vulnerable space during an important conversation. The outcome of this kind of conversation, while you are in this kind of space, may feel vulnerable, but it actually makes for a better outcome. You will be better able to sense small emotional shifts in your teen and respond to them more effectively when you are properly situated to really listen.

Trying to access your quiet space for the first time while you're jumping into a high-stakes conversation about sexuality with your teen is unlikely to have the positive outcome that I'm describing here. Instead, work your way up. Find your space during a conversation where you listen to your teen talk about her difficulty with a teacher, making decisions about time management, what to eat for breakfast—something that will be less emotionally charged for you.

Ultimately, you need to trust yourself in this process of

learning how to listen really well. You have the capacity to do this. You may just have some habits that get in the way of really listening. Some of the problems or detrimental habits that come up when parents are trying to listen to their teenagers include the following:

1. Listening to your own thoughts rather than hers.

2. Fretting or worrying about what she might say.

3. She talks so much—your attention just fades after a little while.

These are things that pull someone out of their quiet space. Let's go through each of them.

You're Listening to Your Own Thoughts Rather Than Hers

It's easy for your own thoughts and internal dialogue to unintentionally take over. You're listening, thinking about what your teenager is saying, and your mind ends up rambling down a tangent. Maybe you're still thinking about the things she's talking about, but on your own terms. Instead of thinking about what she's actually saying, you're considering what to say next or how to make a point you think is important. Parents often do this because they feel uncomfortable with the silence if they wait to think about what to say until their teen has stopped talking. The thing to remember is that it's really OK for there to be silence during conversation (I talked about this in chapter 3).

The thing about listening is that it's more of a feeling that comes from deep inside you than it is an action. Consider the epigraph at the beginning of this chapter. It speaks to the

feeling—rooted deep inside you—that you are in a quiet place rather than a place of cognitive motion and considering what comes next. If you aren't in that internal space, you're not really listening in a deeply attentive way.

There are additional and strong cultural tendencies that make it more likely that parents will listen to their own internal dialogue rather than listening to their teens talk about sex and sexuality. Our culture teaches that the expected dynamic between parents and teenagers is that the teen needs to be constantly reminded of the importance of listening to the parental voice of wisdom. Parents can get in a habit of waiting for the moment to share the voice of wisdom with their teen. This is far from what teenagers need. In fact, the exact opposite is generally true. This is a theme that will come up over and over again in this book. Teenagers need space in their lives to learn and fail. They need a few years to consider their parents' positions on things (which they already—mostly—know) and see if they feel right or not. They need to be listened to.

The act of listening to your teen gets even more difficult

when you add the subject of sex or sexuality into the mix. This topic is very challenging for most people—even when they're talking with adults and about adult sexuality. Adolescent sexuality is even harder for us to grapple with on a cultural level. The messaging about appropriate sexual behavior is pervasive and somewhat contradictory: Be sexy but not too sexy! Abstinence only, until marriage! Use condoms! And so forth! Quieting those cultural messages playing in your head when your teen—the one you know and love—is talking with you is hard! And necessary.

Increasing your skills in listening to your teen takes time and attention. It's a process of realizing that you've drifted into your own thoughts, and gently refocusing on your teen and what she is saying. Learning to let your internal thoughts roll away rather than focusing on them isn't a fast process, and you can't expect it to be. Breaking your old habit of listening to an internal dialogue and building a new habit of focusing on your teen will eventually happen. Be kind, gentle, and accept a slow transition between listening styles. You will get there!

You're Worried about What She Might Say

This is very common, not only for parents of teenagers who are talking about sex, but for all people when someone may be about to say something that is scary, unwelcome, or challenging. It takes practice, and even internal reminders, to release your fear of what might be coming. Maybe it will be what you are worried about. Maybe it will be something else entirely, something good even! Maybe it will be far worse—something you hadn't even considered yet.

The point is that you don't know. You can't know. And worrying and gaming out your potential reaction to something that might happen only serves to distract you from what is actually being said. A friend describes this sort of thing as "living in the wreckage of the future." When you're doing that, in a future that is inherently unknown, you miss much of the now.

If you find yourself tangled up with fears while you are in a conversation with your teen, think back to chapter 1. Your work in that chapter was all about setting your fears aside, but that doesn't mean that they've gone away. Your current conversation may be triggering your fears—or bringing up new ones.

The process to respond to these fears is very much like the process to respond to your internal thoughts. Every time you notice that you are drifting into a fear-based emotional space, or are already in that space, take a deep breath. Mentally bring yourself into the moment, and then back into that quiet listening space inside you. You can take the time to figure out how to react when you have heard your teenager say the things she wants or needs to say. It's OK for there to be silence while you process what she's said.

She Talks So much — Your Attention Just Fades After a Little While

I love teenagers. I started my work in sexuality because I wanted to work with this age group specifically. And even so, there are some teenagers who can talk and talk and talk to the point where your listening stamina is exhausted. Some teenagers have a special skill set for talking. It's a combination of verbal acuity, self-engagement, and developing social awareness that all come together in a seemingly never-ending avalanche of words. (Not all teenagers, of course. Plenty of them don't talk at all. But the ones who talk a lot are hard to listen to completely all of the time.) When even the people who choose to spend large portions of their day with talkative teenagers wear thin sometimes, the rest of humanity must wear thin even faster.

Cut yourself a break every now and then if you have one of those very talkative teens. You've got to plan out dinner some time, and that time might just be when your teen is around and talking. If that's the case, try and include your

teen in the dinner planning, so you'll be talking and thinking about the same thing that she's talking and thinking about. This requires the fewest can-you-please-say-that-agains.

What I am asking of you—to listen from the quiet parts in you to the quiet parts in others—is no small thing, even though it fits on my book-signing stamp. Rather, it is a courageous and remarkable act to listen well in this way. Learning to hear what your teenager's quiet place is saying will provide you with information, deep connection, and renewed intimacy. You'll be able to understand her desires, motivations, and decisions on a deeper level. These things will provide you with guidance on how to ask your one question (see the next chapter!). Indeed, to truly listen to your teenager is more of a gift to yourself than it is a gift to her, because it makes your job as a parent more specific, unique, and tailored to your teen's specific needs.

When You and Your Teen Talk

This is the meat of the rules, in a general sense. This is where you will learn how to handle yourself once conversations about sexuality are actually taking place between you and your teen. This is the most challenging of the three sections.

The three chapters in this section are:

5. You Get One Question
6. Do Something—Anything!—Else
7. Pleasure and Pain

I will go into the details of these rules in the following three chapters. The thing to remember about them is that they are goals to move toward, not absolutes to stress out over achieving immediately. Your work in the first section prepared you to begin to pay attention to these rules, but that doesn't mean that this process will be an easy one. Even I have to come back and reread these rules sometimes to remind myself of their importance.

These are not, of course, the only things you will be doing when you're having a conversation with your teen—but they are meaningful and useful supports for the advice that is typically given. You should, of course, be compassionate, provide information, and offer support. Your ability to read what your teen wants with respect to physical contact, revisiting the subject matter at a different time, and bringing other people into the conversation are all relevant pieces of an effective communication puzzle. The three rules here are tools that augment, support, and develop an even richer line of communication.

You Get One Question

To pause, wait, and consider is to offer the gift
of the space between the stars
so that the brightest one can shine.

I've alluded to this one-question rule in the previous chapters, and now we're going to talk about how the one-question rule works, when it applies, and how to formulate the question. It's important to remember that this is just one question. One question is not very many questions.

It's not actually, literally, absolutely one question ever. Questions about little daily things (like "What time should I pick you up from school?" and "Can you please take out the trash?" and "How was the movie?") don't count. No, this rule is about the big questions, the questions you have emotional investment in. If you find yourself getting worked up about what your teen's potential answer might be, that's when it's time to step back and apply this rule. And the rule is as simple as it sounds: you get one big question, your teen gets a chance to answer (or not), and that's it. No pressure. No pushing. No answer-me-or-I'll-take-away-your-Wi-Fi-password. None of that. The one-question rule works through your discipline of yourself. Let's talk about why.

WHY ONE QUESTION?

There are two reasons that I have found that focusing on just one question is very effective.

1. The one-question rule stops parents from violating the third (Stop Talking) and fourth (Start Listening) rules by taking over the conversation with a barrage of questions.

Sometimes parents get in a (bad) habit of asking a long string of questions without waiting for their teenagers to catch a breath, much less begin to formulate a proper answer. The onslaught of questions sounds something like this: "What's this? Is this a condom? What do you need a condom for? Are you sleeping with that boy? I'm going to kill him! Does he know I'm going to kill him? Just wait until your father gets home! He's going to kill him, too! Is that what you were doing when you were late for curfew the other night when you told us you were going to the movies? [2 second pause in the tirade.] Answer me! Why aren't you answering me?"

The experience of having your parent ask a ream of

questions, all of them relatively big and potentially requiring an attentive and well-phrased response, is overwhelming and ends up being extraordinarily counterproductive for the immediate purposes of the conversation. A teen faced with rapid-fire questions has a hard time formulating the answers and by the end isn't even sure which question to answer first. Furthermore, if the teenager is aware that a potentially explosive subject like sexuality is at hand, he will probably want to gather his thoughts in order to respond well. Giving your teenager the space to answer questions fully and with thought will give you much more insight into his thinking process and what he really wants. It is also far more respectful of him. In addition to this short-term goal, approaching the conversation with a limit of one question will also aid your long-term goal of effective and increased parent-teen communication around topics of sexuality. When your teenager knows that you will be respectful and will not demand immediate answers to a tirade of questions, he will feel more comfortable both coming to you and responding when you come to him.

2. The one-question rule makes parents think very, very carefully about their question.

I have heard parents ask their teenagers a lot of bad questions in my time. Two classic examples of poorly worded parental questions are "Was that really a good idea?" and "If Susan jumped off a bridge, would you jump too?" The problem with both of these questions is that neither of them is really a question. Rather, they are statements of the parent's opinion that the teenager's actions were not well thought out. Also, both of these questions allow a yes-or-no answer, allowing the teenager to effectively end the conversation. By spending more time formulating a really good question rather than falling back on these clichés, you will find that your question opens up space for dialogue and will lead you and your teenager into conversation rather than closing the door on it.

One other lovely side effect of asking parents to formulate one really good question is that they have to take some time to do it. You are far more likely to stop talking when you are trying to figure out a poignant, meaningful question to ask. When you are limited to just one question, you are also far more likely to really listen to what your teenager is telling you in order to prepare yourself to ask the most important question.

WHEN DO I NEED TO ONLY ASK ONE QUESTION?

The short answer is, any time you feel the need to ask your teenager more than one question about sexuality or romance.

The long answer is a bit more complicated. There are three situations when this rule is most useful and applicable. The first is when you want to approach your teenager about a complicated or charged topic or issue. The second is when your teenager approaches you about a complicated or charged topic. The third is when something unexpected pops up. The utility of the one-question rule is a little bit different in each of the scenarios, but nevertheless highly applicable to all.

When approaching your teenager: When you approach your teenager with a topic about sexuality or romance, you need to tread carefully--or maybe I should say thoughtfully. As teenagers develop across the adolescent spectrum, their ideas, morals, and ethical positions are emerging. Adolescence is a difficult time to ask anyone to nail down his beliefs and expect those beliefs to remain unchanged. Given the evolving moral development and deepening of thought that teens experience, coupled with emotional and physical reactions to and around sexuality, conversations about sex have the potential to be uncomfortable and awkward. Sometimes teens just try to get out of those conversations because they're emotionally exhausted.

Nevertheless, sometimes those conversations need to happen regardless of the discomfort. The best way to approach a topic as charged as sexuality is by being straightforward and incredibly gentle. It is the gentleness that applies here. One well-formed question about sexuality or romance is just about as much as most teenagers are able to handle from their parents at one time. You will be showing your teenager respect by approaching him with only one question at a time. You will also be reducing your teenager's anxiety, stress, and other negative reactions to conversations with you about sex. This will provide you and your teenager with a much higher likelihood of future conversations about sexuality and romance.

When your teenager approaches you: It's a sacred moment when your teen comes to talk with you about sex

and sexuality, and it needs to be respected. As someone who is approached often—daily—with questions about sex and sexuality, I see how much trust and bravery is involved in that moment of reaching out. Even adults struggle with it.

You need to honor that moment of trust by responding with quiet openness. The thing about questions is that they lead and direct the conversation rather than following the other person's lead. When your teen comes to you, he needs to be the one leading and directing the conversation. Your teen may be looking for many different things, and it's not always immediately apparent what those are. You'll need to put the listening skills you learned in chapter 4 to good use in order to discover what it is that your teenager is looking for from you. The likelihood that your teen is looking for you to ask him questions is pretty small.

When something unexpected comes up: The third category of situations where the one-question rule applies is when you find out something about your teenager's sexual activities or romantic involvement that you did not know and that you do not approve of. Another way to think about it is that this rule is here to catch you when you're in a parental emotional free fall. It is something to latch on to, intellectually and emotionally, that will give you direction and purpose in staying present and appropriate in your conversation with your teenager.

This last kind of situation is one where this rule is most needed. When you find out or suspect that your teenager has made a decision about sexual or romantic involvement in a way that is upsetting to you, you may be tempted to start off by telling him that you disapprove. This is not helpful, for either your relationship or your teen's decision-making process. As I mentioned earlier, your teenager likely already knows that you will disapprove, because your teenager has a deep understanding of your beliefs about adolescent sexuality and romance. Your goal in these times is to listen to your teenager (chapter 5) as he processes his experiences and choices and then listen to him some more as he processes how he will make decisions and take action in the future.

And you get one question to help you do all of that. It's a tall order, I know. But you can absolutely do it, and you will find it amazingly effective.

HOW DO I GO ABOUT CREATING THAT ONE, IMPORTANT QUESTION?

There are lots of ways to do this, and you'll need to find the approach with which you feel most comfortable. Here are some suggestions, but don't feel like you're limited to what I've included here! Whatever works best for you will be just fine.

1. **Tell your teenager you need some time to think** about what he has said. Brainstorm all of the questions you would like to ask, in whatever language they

bubble up. After you have a list, go back and circle the good questions that will lead to conversation. Notice which ones are not as useful or are more about blaming or stating your own opinion rather than asking a real question. Whittle down your list of questions until you've found the best of the bunch.

2. **Write down your questions** while your teenager talks and either circle the good ones as you go or reread them later. The upside of this process is that you get to capture those questions on paper as you go, and then you may be more likely to move past them and attend to what your teenager is saying rather than mentally focusing on any given point. The potential downside is that this may make your teenager really nervous. Perhaps reassure him that you're only keeping your fidgety hands busy, but your mind attentive to what he's saying. You may also want to let him know that you'll shred the papers afterward.

3. Keep a generally good, nonspecific question tucked away in the back of your mind. This way you'll never have to think under pressure, and you'll always be able to continue the conversation without having to go away, gather your thoughts, and return later. (Although you can both have a standard catchall question for the immediate response and then still go away and come back later to extend the conversation.)

Here are a few general tips on how to formulate and execute one really great question:

1. Create and use open-ended, nonjudgmental questions such as "What else happened?" and "How did that make you feel?"

2. You've got a really great question. Be sure your tone and delivery are really great (i.e., open and nonjudgmental), as well.

3. If you can stay away from making this question sound too much like a therapist's question, that is best. Use words and phrasing that sound natural to you.

And now we're going to get both a little more personal and a little more general. Being able to ask really good questions is an important skill that takes development. Here are a few things to think about as you're building your skill set.

There is beauty to this process of deeply considering your words before you let them fly into the space between you and your teenager. It's not something that's commonly suggested as a way to ease a difficult conversation, but it can be very effective. If you find yourself bogged down at this point or are feeling overwhelmed at the idea of digging into this one-question theory, jump ahead to chapter 10 (all of section

3, really) and read it. Let it sink in. When you're ready, come back to this chapter. It'll be waiting for you when you're in a good state of mind to consider your options.

WHEN DO I GET A SECOND QUESTION?

You're on board, you've created a great question, and you've posed it.

Now what?

I'm glad you've asked!

After your question comes, hopefully, a conversation. You and your teen chatting, with you staying focused on your teen (chapter 2), listening more than you talk (chapters 3 and 4), maybe doing something while you chat (chapter 6), incorporating both the good and the bad about sexuality (chapter 7), and being open to scary topics (chapter 8). When this happens, you're really living the dream! Stay in the moment, be present, and enjoy the ride. Your next big question will come when it's time for another big conversation. That might be an hour or a day or a week or a year away. It's OK to just relax into this process.

There are, of course, a number of ways your teen might respond to your carefully considered question that wouldn't feel nearly as good as having that conversation. Your teen may ignore you, start talking about something else, or give a noncommittal answer. Your teen may roll his eyes, ask why you would ask such a stupid question, or turn around and walk away. If your teen doesn't respond well to your question, that's an invitation for you to continue thinking about and building even better questions.

It's a risk, building up a question like this. But it's an important one, because it has the potential payoff of that dreamy conversation, and there is not really a downside. If your teen rolls his eyes at you now, he probably would have rolled his eyes at you regardless of what you said. That's really more about him and his internal space than it is about you.

If you get brushed off and it's a topic that needs to be talked about, you have a few options. You can spend more time thinking of another question, you can tell your teen that you'll let the conversation go for the moment but that it can't be ignored indefinitely, or you can use the same question again sometime later. Which one of these paths you take depends on the details of your situation. Ask yourself whether you're being as attentive as possible. Are you being sensitive to your teen's needs about when, where, and how you ask your question? How can you ease the process of talking about something difficult? Listen to your gut feelings.

If you're brushed off again, you can ask a follow-up question along the lines of "Is there a way that I can make this topic easier for us to talk about?" or "When is a better time or place for us to talk about this?"

But those are responses that should be used sparingly. They are really designed for critical, top-level conversations. If your teen doesn't want to talk about something (as evidenced by not responding to your question) and you don't feel strongly about having the conversation, let it go for a while. Come up with a new approach. Casually raise the topic again in a few days. If you continue to get pushback on a topic that you wouldn't classify as critical, let it go. Your teen is coming into adulthood, where more privacy and space between parents and children is fully appropriate. Let him stake out his places of privacy and independence.

Do Something – Anything! – Else

*Conversation is an act of creation;
it need not stand alone*

Conversations with your teenager about sex, sexuality, and romance can be easier if the two of you are doing something in addition to the conversation at hand, where you don't have to look at each other. Depending on your personal preferences and those of your teen, grab anything from your knitting to your golf clubs. Just get something (anything!) in front of your eyes and her eyes, so you don't have to look at each other's eyes while you say words like "orgasm" and "vagina."

PICK THE ACTIVITY

Start by picking an activity that your teenager actually enjoys. This is a time to manage your own emotions, consider your teenager's feelings, and put your teenager's feelings first. To allow your teenager to get the most out of the conversation, you need to think clearly about her comfort level. What does she enjoy doing that you can take part in and that will allow a conversation to go on simultaneously? Here are some ideas:

- Playing games (computer, console, role playing, board games, etc.)
- Sports (basketball or playing catch are prime examples)
- Running, walking, or hiking (make sure your pace allows for conversation)
- Cooking (something that your teenager will want to eat)
- Driving (through the country or on your daily routine)

Note that all of these activities are ones where you and your teenager will remain in relatively close physical proximity to each other, you can talk and be heard, and you don't have to look each other in the eye. Within these parameters, almost any activity your teenager likes will suffice.

START THE CONVERSATION

Parents are often aware of conversation topics they want to discuss with their teenagers about sexuality and romance. Sometimes parents feel awkward starting those conversations. This section is a crash how-to course on starting conversations about sex with your teenager. The conversation will probably still feel awkward. You may stutter. You may be embarrassed and blushing. All of those things are OK. Making sure the conversation happens, and that you stay present for the entire thing is far more important.

After you're set up in your activity comes the hard part. No teenager (or adult, really) wants to hear those dreaded four words: "We need to talk." So don't say them and don't start with the hard conversation. Instead, begin with a neutral conversation. Something that will, hopefully, open up the conversation floor, something you know that your teenager is interested in. Recent activities? Sports? Computer or console games? Music? Books? Friends? Food? Anything, really. The point is that it's something they enjoy and can get them talking.

After you and your teenager are doing whatever it is you're doing and have started a friendly conversation, gently push the conversation toward your conversational goal, whatever that is. This is a really good place to use that one question you've thoroughly planned. (Go back to chapter 5 if you want more support in finding that question.)

You might come across as ob-

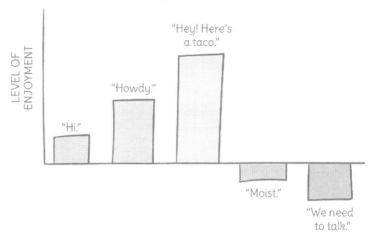

Reactions to Hearing Common Words & Phrases

vious; your teenager might even see right through the whole charade of a one-on-one activity (especially if you haven't started doing them regularly yet!) and an easy conversation opener as a way to get her comfortable talking before you bring up the heavy subjects. And that's OK, as long as you have times when you hang out and do things with your teenager that she wants to do, when you do not bring up heavy subjects. Your teenager shouldn't be under the impression that you only engage in "her" activities when you have a conversation agenda.

This actually leads to a point that I often try to make with parents: engaging in an activity with your teenager (that she enjoys) at least once a week will dramatically improve your relationship. This is a little like the advice to eat at least one meal per day together as a family, but it is more focused on what your teenager wants to do—and may be more effective in the long run at solidifying your relationship and thus your ability to have heavy conversations on topics like sex.

Try to do one of your starred activities with your teen every week, whether you have important conversations during them or not. It will normalize the activities and make them less surprising or awkward when you need to find a time to have a more personal conversation.

Once your one-question starter has happened, follow your teenager's lead. If she's not in the mood for a conversation, that will be clear. You can let her know that you want to have the conversation at some point, but it doesn't have to be right then. If she takes you up on the offer, plan another time for the heavy conversation. And then stay and continue having lighter conversations and enjoying your activity with your teen. If she is going to trust your presence in her life as meaningful, you can't make her feel that you are only interested in hard conversations. There have to be fun times, too, and on her terms.

The Rhythm of Conversation

Conversations can ebb and flow—particularly when there is something else that is also happening. If you're playing a game, for example, the conversation will pause to accommodate conversation about the game play, rules, and turns. If you're cooking, it will be about ingredients. If you're playing basketball, it will be during the faster paced moments of the game. Those pauses—the moments of focus on other things—are part of why doing something else while you're talking is useful. It gives you both a moment to breathe, release any intensity, and think about what you've said and heard. Use these moments rather than being annoyed or feeling distanced because of them.

The end of the conversation may happen differently, too. If you're doing a discrete activity that clearly has an ending point, and you haven't finished your conversation, that might leave you not quite sure what to do next. It's OK to let the conversation end here, too, even if it wasn't a natural ending place. You can come back to the conversation again another time. As an adult regularly involved in your teen's life, you have the benefit of engaging with them regularly and having access to ongoing, evolving conversations over days or even weeks.

Or you can move on to some other activity. Or maybe you and your teen have become more comfortable with the conversation itself and can be more comfortable just talking (listening). There are lots of possibilities. See what feels the most natural in the moment.

What to Do When Your Teen Doesn't Appear to Be Listening

You've got a conversation going, but it's all one way? You feel like you're talking to a black hole? You're trying to shed some light, but everything you say is getting sucked in and nothing is coming back out at you? You have no idea if your teenager is even listening, much less understanding or agreeing with your little minilecture on safe sex or drugs or the importance of getting good grades? These are trying times. These are the times when parents stop talking with their teenagers because they don't want to continue to pour energy into talking to someone who's not listening.

And you should stop talking.

But not because your teen isn't listening.

You should stop talking because lecturing isn't achieving your goal.

Because really, your teenager already knows your opinions on drugs or grades or sex or whatever else it is. (No, yes, safely, etc.)

Even if she appears to have unexpectedly turned herself into a black hole, it's OK. She already knows what it is you're saying.

As a parent, you have a disproportionate amount of power and influence over your teen. You know this from when she was young—young children imitate their parents incessantly. Now that your child has grown into a teenager, she is working to differentiate herself from you and the rest of her family of origin. She may try to actively push you away or she may just try to ignore you. But trust that, deep within her, she is not ignoring you. You and your thoughts, feelings, values, and opinions are still part of her. You are still one of the most important people in her life, and the only way that can change is if you stop believing it.

There are a couple of common mistakes that parents make around this point. Some parents just get discouraged by the lack of feedback. Other parents get overzealous and talk louder and longer, hoping that will help. Really, neither of these is a good approach. In order to maximize the influence your words and opinions have with your teenager, you need to minimize them. You have to use your words and your thoughts very, very sparingly. Each single sentence that you say burrows down inside your teenager and wiggles around, bumping up against your teenager's private thoughts and feelings. Use that power wisely, and you will find it has great effect.

Just one question. That's all it takes. If the conversation doesn't get off the ground, it clearly wasn't the right time. Give it a few days and bring it up again in a different way.

What about Texting?

Sometimes both teenagers and parents find texting to be an easier way to have difficult conversations, for many of the same reasons that simultaneously engaging in some other behavior offers: not being too physically close, not being overwhelmed, and so forth.

Whether you should use texting in this way really depends on you and your teen. If it works for you, by all means run with it! If it's something you've never tried but think

If you're going to have sex with Devon, just be sure to use colons

*cantaloupes

*Comfort Inns

*CONDOMS

Beware the Autocorrect

might work, give the process a test run with a topic that's low key rather than high stakes. If texting is something that your teen is highly engaged in (many are, but some aren't), it's worth at least exploring. Texting is itself a language, with rhythms and pauses and ways to provide depth of meaning that can happen more naturally sometimes than in face-to-face conversations. It should not necessarily be written off as a form of holding difficult conversations, if it is the form of communication that comes most easily to your teen.

WHEN YOUR TEENAGER STARTS THE CONVERSATION

Thus far, I've only addressed parent-started conversations. These are the ones you can plan for, which means these are the ones you have the most control over. When your teen approaches you, however, there can be different reactions and emotions to process, and you can't get ahead of the process by doing that beforehand. It's important to note that when you approach your teen, she has the same set of issues to grapple with; you need to be patient with her as she does that.

Sometimes parents are blindsided by their teenager starting a conversation about sex. Too often this is because the teenager finds herself in need of help—either because of a pregnancy or an STD—and parents aren't prepared to hear that their teen is having sex at all, much less dealing with its negative ramifications. But regardless of the reason why she is reaching out, when a teenager comes to talk with a parent about sexuality, it is the parent's responsibility to listen and engage.

Before your teenager comes to talk with you about something like this, it is useful for parents to consider how they might engage with her. Here are a few tips: In chapter 2, I talked about the focus of conversations being on the teenager; chapters 3 and 4 covered how to give your teenager your full attention. These things, of course, continue to apply here. However, in addition to giving focus to your teen and listening well, you might find that it is easier to have a difficult conversation like this while your hands or body are doing something else. The activities from the first section in this chapter apply here as well, but they are a bit broader if your teen is starting the conversation. If you are already engaged in some way—washing dishes, gardening, and so forth—it is fine to continue that activity for the duration of the conversation. You can even hand your teenager something to keep her hands busy while you talk. She chose this time to approach you. If it's possible, open up your activity to include her.

If you are doing something that can't really continue while you talk (reading, watching a movie, showering), wrap up what you're doing as quickly as you can and find something to keep both of your hands busy. If there is nothing easily at hand, ask your teenager if she wants to go for a walk or a drive while you talk, and then stay present. If you're finding that difficult, see chapters 9 and 10. They'll give you support for engaging when the engagement gets tough.

If the conversation gets emotionally intense, you may find yourself naturally putting down what you are doing and focusing more exclusively on your teen. Let this process between conversation and activity wax and wane naturally. Allow time to pull over, be late to your destination, sit down during the hike, pause the game and finish it after the talk lightens again.

It's also true that if you play your cards right, you can get the dishes done, the floors swept (although not vacuumed—that's too loud), the errands run, and the laundry folded and put away, all while talking with your teen. And that's a win for sure!

Pleasure & Pain

The heights and the depths,
they both hold truths.

With the rules in this book, you have opened doors for your teenager to talk with you, and, hopefully, you're finding those doors creaking open (or—even better!—remaining open). As a result, conversations you were unprepared to have may be coming up. This and the following chapters are all about coping with the conversations you've made space for.

Sexuality involves emotions that span human experience—the good, the bad, the transcendent, the surprising, the scarring. Sexuality touches on each of these feelings and many more. The kinds of experiences that come from a positive sexual experience are life enhancing. They build up our ideas of ourselves, those we love, and what is possible in our lives. They make us stronger, more engaged, more human. A negative sexual experience can pull us physically, emotionally, and psychologically into the dark depths.

Young people are often confused, and rightfully so, by the ways they learn about sex and sexuality. They hear the sexually good and the sexually bad discussed in very different ways. Socially based media messages are more likely to exclusively focus on the potential positive effects of sexuality—the physical pleasure—without addressing the potential for pregnancy, STI transmission, heartbreak, rape, or more. On the other hand, educational contexts focus primarily on these very negatives without contextualizing them within the positives—human connection, touch, attraction, and love.

This chapter addresses the need to integrate the positive and negative potentials of sexuality into family-based conversations. Teenagers need support to understand how to negotiate the pulls between the many valid and competing emotions and potential outcomes around sexual decision

making. And so, you must talk about the pleasure sex can bring as well as the pain. And you have to let your teenager talk about it as well. Yes, that means you may have to talk about orgasms and hear your teenager say something like, "It feels good when Jessie…"

Figuring out how to bring pleasure into your conversations is no small thing—nor is it something that is typically supported by the culture around us. Even though teenagers know that part of why people want to have sex is because of the physical pleasure and psychological connectedness, it is still taboo to talk about those things with them. But you won't be telling them anything they don't know. I hope you'll come along for the ride with me, and at least withhold judgment on this particular point until you've read the rest of the chapter.

HOW PLEASURE IS GENERALLY LEFT OUT OF THE SEX CONVERSATION

Family conversations about sex and sexuality tend to focus on one of two things (or potentially both things, over time and depending on circumstance):

- Why, and how, to say no to having sex
- Why, and how, to use condoms or other forms of birth control

And these are great! Important! Very important! But they are not the only important things.

In fact, most of this book has been opening the floor in order for teenagers to have the space to talk about all of the other things that arise in conversations about sexuality: love, confusion, arousal, identity, and so forth. These are gateway conversations to the real nitty-gritty of sexuality. But they are also messy and confusing. They lack clarity of purpose and introduce misperception and misunderstanding into conversations. They are intimidating when compared to clearly formed, clearly articulable points like: Don't have sex. Use a condom. Date someone who's nice to you. Don't get an STI.

In reality, the entry conversations about sexual pleasure are usually not even yet begun.

WHY TALKING ABOUT PLEASURE IS IMPORTANT

Honesty in all topics relating to sexuality is the one tool parents have that makes the most difference in whether the teenagers respect parental thoughts or ignore them. When someone discounts an entire range of emotion about an experience, it's easy to discount what they say about the rest of the experience. It's easy to think that they're naïve, mimicking, not being real.

This problematic dynamic is very similar to the drug education that suggests anyone who does any form of drug will have his life fall apart around him. When the teenager sees others smoking pot, and realizes that their lives did not fall apart around them, the suggestion that all drugs lead directly to a downward spiral is disproved. The problem is that some drugs may lead directly into a downward spiral for some, but an all-or-nothing education leads students to lump all drugs into one category—they are either life threatening or else not really drugs. As long as a teenager has no knowledge of any person who does any drug and isn't dramatically affected by it, he can continue to believe that all drugs are life threatening. But zero experience is uncommon in most communities, and Internet access makes it virtually impossible to remain unexposed to information about drugs and drug use.

And so, the same basic line of thought holds true for conversations about sex and sexuality. When teenagers see that sexual activities don't have to have negative side effects—indeed, they can even be pleasurable!—they can come to discount even the accurate pieces of information they have.

WHY TALKING ABOUT PAIN IS IMPORTANT

Most people have an intuitive sense of why it is important to talk about the more difficult areas of sex and sexuality: because young people need to know how and where and why and when things might go wrong, to be warned against the potential hurts, both physical and emotional. But the need goes much deeper than that.

A teenager needs his parents to bring up the hard topics about sexuality (not just STIs and unplanned pregnancy, but also rape, abuse, and emotional loss) so that he doesn't have to. If a teenager has never had a conversation with his parents about sexual assault, for example, he is going to have a much harder time going to them for help if he experiences (or commits) a sexual assault. However, if he is aware of his parents' perspectives on sexual assault, and feels like it is a safe conversation to have, there is more room for him to reach out for help. Beginning a conversation about something as difficult as STIs, unplanned pregnancy, or someone breaking your heart is hard enough when a teenager knows that his parent will support him however he needs support. If he doesn't know how his parent will react, it is exponentially more difficult.

A teenager who knows that his parents will listen, believe, love, and support him in his experiences is safer, because he has backup when he is in need. That kind of knowledge can only come in a family that talks about the painful aspects of sexuality openly and honestly. Conversations about sexual pain are really about painful experiences—times when you will need to come together as a family to support each other.

They are a bellwether for whether your teen will come to you and what kind(s) of support you have to offer during the potentially most trying and emotional parts of his life.

HOW TO INCLUDE PLEASURE

Because it has typically been ignored in conversations about sex and sexuality, most of us don't have a blueprint of how to include pleasure in a conversation about sex. But, hopefully, we agree that it's important. Now that you're ready to move beyond the theoretical, your first step will be to acknowledge that this process may not be easy (for you or the teen you'll be talking with eventually).

To help you get over this internal barrier, I have five steps. Start on these at whatever place you feel is most appropriate for you. If even privately acknowledging sexual pleasure is new for you, start at step one. If you have thought about sexual pleasure, but never verbalized those thoughts, start at step 2. If talking about pleasure is fairly accessible to you, then go directly to step 4 and start planning your conversation with your teen. I have included a little detail about how to accomplish each of these steps.

Five Steps to Learning to Talk about Pleasure

1. Think about sexual pleasure.
2. Talk about sexual pleasure with an adult.
3. Have a conversation with a second adult.
4. Write several sentences you feel you can say to your teenager about sexual pleasure.
5. Find the time and the place to say at least one of your preplanned sentences to your teenager.

Let's delve more deeply into how to take each of those steps. This can be a slow process—it might take a year, or even more, for sexual pleasure to become a comfortable topic for you to talk about.

Step 1: Think about sexual pleasure. You will not be able to talk with anyone else about sexual pleasure until you acknowledge it within yourself. It is important that you are, at the very least, able to say the word aloud when you are alone. Beyond that, figure out what you think about sexual pleasure. Think about your history of sexual pleasure. How have past sexual experiences been for you, in terms of pleasure? Writing a series of journal entries about your personal experiences with and relationship to pleasure is a lovely way to begin your journey into understanding sexual pleasure on a personal level.

Step 2: Talk about sexual pleasure with an adult. The move from thinking and writing about pleasure by yourself to having the conversation aloud, which includes saying potentially difficult words aloud to another person, can be quite hard. In order to ease the difficulty of this transition, the most obvious person to talk about pleasure with is your current sexual partner, if you have one. If you are talking with your sexual partner, talk about your own sex life. What feels good to you, what feels good to them. If you don't have a current sex partner, talk with a close friend. Your conversation obviously won't be as personal, but it will still be very useful.

Step 3: Have a conversation with a second adult. Now that you've talked with one adult about sexual pleasure, talk with another! This process will, hopefully, get easier—or at least more familiar—with each conversation you have. By now you have moved your conversation beyond your current sexual partner. Make sure you have also moved the topic of conversation to pleasure in a more general sense, rather than the specifics of your own sexual preferences. Remember chapters 1 and 2: know yourself well enough to remember that it's not about you!

Step 4: Write four or five sentences you feel you can say to your teenager about sexual pleasure. Memorize them. Say them aloud to yourself, say them aloud to at least the two other adults with whom you have already had conversations about sexual pleasure. Get their feedback. Now plan for a time (1) when you think you might be able to work your sentences into natural conversation, or (2) to be with your teenager and have a more formal conversation about pleasure. Whenever possible, I recommend the first option.

Step 5: Find the time and the place to say at least one of your preplanned sentences to your teenager. See how it goes. This will be a learning experience for both of you. After the initial foray into a conversation about pleasure, you will have an idea of how to proceed the next time. Maybe your conversation starter fell flat—if your teenager was embarrassed or did not engage, don't lose heart. Try and try again! (See chapter 10!) The conversations will become less awkward, and your teenager will open up as he sees that you are really engaged and accepting of a conversation about sexual pleasure. If your conversation took off, if your teenager was engaged and had lots of questions and thoughts—great!

Don't let it end there! Ask a follow-up question a few days later to let your teenager know that you have thought about what he had to say and are willing and interested in continuing the conversation.

HOW TO INCLUDE PAIN

While conversations about sexual pain come more easily to many adults than conversations about sexual pleasure, they can prove difficult to have with your own teenager. It seems a little trite to say it, but pain is painful. Talking about sexually painful issues that may make you angry, sad, or lonely, or that may trigger things you've struggled with in your own sexual history, while still keeping the conversation open in the ways that chapters 1 through 6 recommend, is very difficult! But maintaining that openness is exactly what you are being invited to do.

The benefit of staying open is that your teen will come to you when something sexually painful has happened, and he needs you most of all. In those times, pulling in your own emotional reaction and being supportive of your teen is an even bigger emotional challenge. But it's one you've been training for. The steps that you went over to learn how to incorporate sexual pleasure into your conversations are also really useful here. Think about the difficult issue at hand, talk about it with one other adult and then at least one more adult, write it out, and then start the conversation with your teen. You will have an easier time (not to say it will be actually easy, just that it will be easier) talking about the very difficult issues around sex and sexuality if you've gone through these steps.

Chapters 8 and 9 both include specific suggestions about how to maintain a listening, loving, supportive presence during these kinds of conversations with your teen. For now,

I only want to reiterate the importance of those kinds of reactions, as both a practice time for you and a signal to your teen about your potential reaction if something painful or scary or hurtful were to actually happen. During a time of stress, your teen will be particularly vulnerable. He may need your help in any number of ways, both practical and emotional. For him to be able to expect you to react out of love is a huge gift.

Being open to the topics of both sexual pleasure and pain will substantially increase your credibility with your teenager. He will absolutely respect your opinion and moral principles more fully if you are able to acknowledge that sex and sexuality is pleasurable activity *an* convey love and caring for him during conversations about painful outcomes of potentially poor choices.

Don't be afraid to talk about feeling horny and orgasms, in a general sense if not in a personal sense. And don't be afraid that showing your teen love when he is in pain will only serve to encourage poor decision-making in the future. These conversations will deepen your connection with your teenager and will open up your conversations about sex in ways that will surprise you!

The Voice Inside

It is often the case that our internal voices are destructive rather than constructive. It is easy to focus on the little things in ourselves that we see as not quite meeting the standard to which we hold ourselves. This section is designed to push against that trend. Rather than pulling yourself down for not meeting your goals, this section is designed to give you a positive framework for moving forward toward your goals. Rather than feeling bad because in one conversation or another you talked too much or didn't acknowledge an opening to talk about sexual pleasure, this section is here to remind you of the ways you can be brave in the face of the uncomfortable next time around.

The three chapters in this section are:

8. Be Cool As a Cucumber
9. Bring It On
10. Never Surrender

Learning to listen to a positive internal voice, to in fact cultivate that positivity, will allow you to hold difficult conversations more easily because you won't beat yourself up about the small stuff. When you're calling yourself out on every small step outside of an ideal, you will not be able to fully submerge yourself in the process of conversation. Instead, you need positive feedback and recognition for what you have been able to do, and what you will be able to do next time. When you find yourself in need of positive feedback, you will find it here. The last chapter is the most clearly directed at encouraging you when you are feeling down—but the other two also serve that purpose by encouraging a state of mind that is both accepting and brave.

I believe in you—both generally, because I believe in parents' abilities to learn and improve their skills as parents, but also specifically. You picked up this book. You were ready to improve your communication. If you've gotten this far, you've probably been challenged with new ideas, and you've stuck with me. So I believe in you—specifically. You are on an important path of self and relational growth. Keep going!

Be Cool As a Cucumber

I am as deep as the ocean.
I am as timeless as the stones.
I breathe.

If I were to set out a series of goals for your internal, emotional space during conversations with your teenager about sex and sexuality, it would be these:

- Nothing surprises you.
- You access your strength and your stability from the bottomless depths of the ocean.
- You are in the zone.

- You are the embodiment of Zen.

These internal states are really important because the minute you get worked up or have any negative reaction, your teenager will stop talking. Always let her talk herself out—whether that takes two minutes or two hours. If given the time and space to talk, she will process through her own emotions, good and bad. If you're upset about whatever it is she's talking about, it can be hard to just let her talk without expressing your frustration or disappointment. However, many teens will end up being just as hard on themselves as you would have been, with the added benefit of you not having wedged harsh words into the middle of your relationship.

How to accomplish this inner state (and the external embodiment of that state) is deceptively simple. First, just don't talk. Remain silent, but emotionally and thoughtfully connected to your teenager. It's OK to just stay present and wait, through silence or a torrent of words. Your teenager will probably start talking and then stop talking, going back and forth. It may happen all in one sitting or over several days. Eventually your teenager will get all of her thoughts and emotions out. After it's all done—or in between, when she's taking breaks—that's when you let your frustration out to your co-parent(s), a friend, a therapist, a minister, as long as it's someone who is not your teen.

Let's break that down a little bit more, shall we?

YOUR GOAL

Here are two stories about three mothers who reached into their ocean depths of calm when their teenage children brought them heavy conversations:

Story One

A teenage girl and her boyfriend decide to start having

sex. The scene in the kitchen the next morning, with no preamble or warning, goes something like this:

Daughter: "I'm going to start having sex."

(Long, weighty pause.)

Mother: "How far did you get on your college applications last night?"

And the conversation on college applications was off and running. Later that evening, after she had fully composed herself, she came back to her daughter and said, "Tell me more about your decision to start having sex," and let her daughter talk herself out.

Story Two

A young heterosexual couple had sexual intercourse for the first time. The young woman freaked and thought she might be pregnant. Here is how her mother reacted:

Daughter: "Mom, I had sex. I think I might be pregnant."

(Long, weighty pause.)

Mother: "I love you. Tell me about that."

After hours of letting her daughter talk herself out, the mother finally asked, "Have you taken a pregnancy test yet?"

Daughter: "No."

Mother: "Then let's go get you one. I love you."

And here is how the young man involved told his mother while they were out shopping:

Son: "Mom, my girlfriend might be pregnant."

The mother stopped pushing the cart, turned around, and walked out of the store in silence. She drove herself and her son around in silence for half an hour. When she finally took them home, she picked up the basketball in the driveway, shot a basket, and said, "Tell me more."

All of these mothers were suddenly and without warning plunged into a conversation about their children's sexuality that they were emotionally unprepared for. While they all had the option to yell, argue, blame, and more, they chose to step back and open up the floor for their children to talk.

There are other situations that aren't as abrupt, disarming, or high stakes as these examples, such as:

- The first date;
- The first sexy text message;
- The first major holiday your teen wants to spend with the person she's dating;
- The first time you find pornography on your teen's computer or cell phone.

All of these situations, plus many others, require a calm, open reaction when a parent might not be in the best state of mind to offer this kind of response.

WHY IS THIS IMPORTANT?

Parents often vaguely try to do something along the line of remaining calm, but if they haven't fully understood why it is critical to keep their cool, they generally aren't as successful at it. There is nothing more important than remaining calm when something your teenager says or does engenders a big emotional or physical reaction from you. This sentence is so critical that I'm going to say it again to really drive the point home: *There is nothing more important than remaining calm when something your teenager says or ·oes engen·ers a big emotional or physical reaction from you.*

When your teenager opens up to you about something like sex, sexuality, or romance, she is putting a huge amount of trust in you. Even when your teenager is forced to come to talk to you, or when you inadvertently run across something about your teen's love life, she is still put in a position where she must trust you, her parent, to be kind, gentle, and open about her very personal and very intimate thoughts and

Mmhmm.. Tell me more, Honey.

feelings. Showing yourself to be worthy of that tenuous trust will allow it to grow over the years, and will foster open lines of communication.

Some people interpret the phrase "open lines of communication" to mean that the parent wants the teenager to be open about everything she is doing in order for the parent to tell her whether it's OK or not, and then the teenager will do what the parent says. But that's really not what I'm talking about here, because a teenager (particularly an older teenager of sixteen, seventeen, or eighteen) will never choose to participate in open communication if it includes the parent judging or being critical. She would just choose to lie, whether directly or by omission.

When I say "open lines of communication," I mean that the parents have to stop talking, find their Zen place of calm, and listen to their teenager as she embarks on what can be a scary, scary journey. Remember from chapter one, your teenager already knows or can anticipate almost a replica of your opinions and positions on everything having to do with sex. You can check that box, and now it's your turn to listen. And make sure you stay calm while you do it!

Nothing—nothing!—will allow you to provide more support to your teenager than to continue listening to her talk to you. If you don't know what's going on, you won't be able to provide help. If you don't keep your cool, you won't have the gift of knowing what's going on. Find your Zen, keep your cool, sit on your hands, bite your tongue, however you want to phrase it—just do it!

THE HOW

You've got the what and the why; now we're going to delve into the how. There is, of course, the common advice to count to ten before reacting. I take this one step further:

count to ten and then ask your teenager to keep talking.

We can make many assumptions about where our teenagers are coming from when we're talking about sex and romance. A friend's four-year-old asked the innocent question, "Where did I come from, Mama?" My friend was internally putting together a long response that included male and female anatomy and reproductive cycles, partnership, consent, and more. But the girl was just trying to remember which neighbor's house she had just come home from. Thankfully, the mother realized her gross misunderstanding of her daughter's question before she started down her line of explanation about reproduction. Misunderstandings can also happen with teenagers. Sometime they're trying out new words that they don't fully understand and using them incorrectly, sometimes they really are talking about a friend, and sometimes they do know the right thing to do and just need space to talk out a decision they'd rather not be making at all.

The point is that, far too often, we parents jump to conclusions or make assumptions about what our

Workbook
Cooling Your Hot Head

Look back at the scenarios you came up with earlier. Which ones might prompt a hotheaded response from you? How might you respond to each one that would invite your teen to talk more?

When You Need to Vent

Who can you talk with when you need to vent steam, worry, express anxiety, and so on about your teen's sexuality, sexual choices, and more?

107

children and teenagers are telling or asking us. It's far more useful as a parent to stop these initial reactions. Be cool. Take a deep breath. Listen. If you absolutely cannot maintain your calm, put the conversation off until later. And then listen. Hear your teenager out. If it's something that has already happened, there's nothing you can do to change it and there's no point in getting angry. (Blowing off steam can be really important—but there is a time and a place, and this isn't it.) If it's something that is going to happen in the future, there's still time for your teenager to change her mind. Give your teenager the space to change her mind rather than trying to change it for her.

And then comes the fun part—or at least the next step, which gets you closer to a loving, accepting resolution. As you're listening to your teenager, count every time you find that you want to respond, that you want to make clear what you think about something, that you want to judge. Count every time you have to physically close your lips to make sure you do not say anything but, rather, continue to listen.

When your teen is done talking, tell her you love her. Give her a hug. Tell her you want to take some time to think about what she's said. Say you hope she'll continue to think about it, too. Set a time to come back to the conversation. It may need to be relatively soon, like later that day, or it may be able to be put off for a week. You'll probably know how urgent it is to continue the conversation.

Find someone else—your co-parent, your best friend, your sister, your brother, your therapist, or someone like me—and let it all out. You know how many times you wanted to say something in that conversation. Tick off each item to this compassionate third party—let it all out. Yell. Scream. Cry. Worry. Whatever you need to do to get out all of the angst that came up while you were listening to your teen talk, do it.

If you're still worried about whether you will be able to maintain a strong, open conversational front with your teenager, then map out exactly what you're going to say (plan that one question I talk about in chapter 8). Anticipate what your teenager might say in response, and what you might say then. It's OK to tell your teenager that you really want to listen to all of her thoughts on the matter, that you want to hear everything she has to say, and that your goal is to support her and love her. It's OK to be upfront if she asks you what she should do, and say, "I would love to give you all the answers, my dear, to take away all the uncertainty and pain in your life. But you are old enough to start finding your own answers. And I will always be here to listen to you and ask you questions to help you find your own answers." Your teenager will feel the trust and belief you have in her to make the right decisions, and that will influence her far more than you saying she "has to" do whatever you think the best decision is.

Bring it On!

I embody bravery,
inside and out.
I am as unshockable as the stars.

This chapter comes on the tails of chapter 8 because it is necessarily based in the cool, collected self that you have come to embody. Before standing bravely in the face of that which challenges you, you must be grounded in a sense of calm. Being brave is something you can take note of in yourself when you are able to do it, and be proud of it.

In order to engage with your teenager, you must be open and welcoming when he shows any inclination to talking about sexuality in general or his sex life specifically. Even if you're uncomfortable. Even if you feel like he's making horrible choices. The time to bring up those reservations is at a later time, when your teenager isn't in the process of opening up of his own volition and, more importantly, you have a bit more perspective and time to plan out what you're going to say.

Many people—maybe even most people—have a hard time talking honestly about sexuality. Sexuality is a hard topic because our culture is not fully at home with the kind of person-to-person connection we associate with sexual activities. Most conversations about sex come with drama—and a certain puritanical drop of shame. And so, most people do not fully live and accept their own sexuality. Teenagers, of course, feel this particularly acutely, as they are just beginning to discover their sexuality amid this roiling culture of "be sexy but not too sexy." Parents bring their own sexual history (and therefore sexual issues) to the table, but they also bring their own preconceived notions of adolescent sexuality. Feelings of insecurity when talking about sex affect your conversations with your teenagers from two directions—yours and theirs.

Your teenager probably feels shy talking about sex with you. This is normal and to be expected. But you have an investment in helping your teenager move past that embarrassment in order to be open with you about his relationships and sexual activity. For your teenager to move through his initial discomfort, you will have to move through your discomfort first.

It's not easy (or...er...comfortable) to move through the places that make you nervous about sex and sexuality. When I first started teaching sex ed to teenagers, I was not as well informed as I am now about all of the varieties of sexual interests that abound in this world. Similarly, I was not as experienced in answering the amazing questions that young people come up with. But I found very quickly that if I was surprised or taken aback when presented with a scenario or a question, the young people in front of me quickly shut down. Teenagers often, above all else, want to appear to be within their own defined range of "acceptable" or "normal." Their sexuality is no different. When my reaction was one of surprise or shock, or when it was apparent I was hearing about a sexual activity or interest for the first time, or even if I was just really uncomfortable talking about it, the teenagers in my classes immediately were forced to wonder whether they were outside the "normal range." And that made them shut down.

As I became more experienced, I found it helpful to read about a huge range of sexual activities from as many different perspectives as I could. The very practical result was that whatever question or scenario teenagers bring to me, I know what they're talking about. Adults say to me, "Wow, you are unshockable!" And that is, in fact, exactly my goal as a sexuality educator.

Being unshockable will need to be your goal as well, as a parent who wants to have conversations with your teenager about sexuali-

Workbook
Uncomfy Subjects

What makes you uncomfortable when thinking about talking with your teen about sex and sexuality? What do you think might make your teen uncomfortable?

113

ty. If your teenager feels that you are in any way shocked or surprised or biting your tongue, he will put on the conversation brakes and head for the hills. Your teenager is putting a lot of trust in you by pushing through his initial discomfort in talking about sex. You will need to honor that trust by pushing through your own insecurities and remaining grounded, focused, unshocked, and completely nonjudgmental.

Achieving this state takes three steps:

1. Harken back to the deep, calm-ocean Zen from chapter 8.
2. Face the discomfort.
3. Invite the discomfort.

This is a process that requires a degree of bravery on your part. If you're struggling with this idea of bravery, read chapter 10. It's there to offer encouragement and support in many ways and for many blocks.

Here is the concern that parents generally offer about facing their discomfort (rule 2): "But I don't know everything about sex, and certainly don't have the time/interest to read enough about it to get me up to speed! How can I do this?"

There are really two points to this answer. First, you do not have to know everything about sex. I certainly do not have an answer at my mental finger tips to every question or situation that comes up with teenagers. It is fine to tell a teenager, or anyone, "Hmm. I need to think on that one. Let's talk again about it tomorrow," or "Oh, I know just the resource to point you to. Let's go look for that book now/call that friend/look that up online." You do not need to be a walking sexual encyclopedia. You just need to be calm.

The calm is possible because you have invited the discomfort in. When you know that there may be awkwardness and embarrassment and when you have accounted for that in your expectations, your reaction to those feelings can be calm. It helps if you also have an idea of where you can look

Auguste Rodin's Lesser Known Work: The Shrugger

for answers to questions that you aren't sure about.

"But you said that the way you learned to be calm was by reading and learning a lot about sexuality! How can I quickly jump to that place?"

Gentle Reader, that's what I am here for. You will need to do some reading and some thinking about sexuality issues to keep your emotional balance and stay open to what your teenager has to say, regardless of what he is bringing to you. To this end, I have compiled a list of topics (along with books and websites available on my website, www.HushFactor. com/resources) that will support your learning. This may be a daunting list. If you feel yourself getting overwhelmed, skip it. You can always come back when you're ready. (This list is organized alphabetically.)

- Abortion
- Acquaintance rape
- Anal intercourse
- Anatomy (the body systems)
- Birth control
- Condoms (access and use)

- Embryology (how fertilization happens)
- Friends with benefits relationships
- Gender identity
- Gender stereotypes
- Masturbation
- Media literacy
- Nonmonogamous relationships
- Normal human bodies (what they look like naked)
- Oral sex
- Orgasm
- Physiology (the way the body systems function)
- Pregnant and parenting teens
- Puberty
- Sexual consent (both requesting and accepting/declining)
- Sexual harassment
- Sexual orientation
- Sexual pleasure
- Sexual slang
- Social media
- STI/STD prevention
- STI/STDs
- Vaginal intercourse

This is not a comprehensive list of topics that your teenager might bring to you. But it's a decent start, and the resources listed on my website can point you to more information about other topics elsewhere.

You do not necessarily need to go read up on each of these topics—now or ever. But I do suggest that you look into the ones you feel particularly uncomfortable with. These are the topics that you will have the hardest time being brave about if your teenager ever needs you to talk about them. Doing a little bit of prep work with your touchiest places is not a bad thing. Of course, if you find yourself suddenly presented with a topic that you were unprepared for, call a time-out, and do your research then.

It is useful to have books in the house and know reputable websites where information about each of these topics can be relatively easy to find—and now you have access to that! If your teenager does have a question that you do not know the answer to, you will be able to find the answer together.

Throughout your child's development, remember that you are your teen's primary sexuality educator. When he was a child, your teen mirrored your actions, language, habits, and more. As a teen, he will continue to mirror you in surprising ways. Conversation between the two of you about sexuality is one of those areas: if you are able to be calm, thoughtful, and measured, your teenager will, too. If your teenager has experience talking about and thinking about sexual issues with you, there is a substantially greater likelihood that he will be able to talk with his sexual partners about it in the same way. Remember the long-term goal: physically and emotion-

Workbook
Finding Resources

What are five resources you can access for more information when talking about sex and sexuality?

Identifying Topics

What are other topics that your teen might be interested in at some point? How would you learn about those topics?

ally healthy adult sexuality. This requires partners who talk about sex together. When you are able to maintain openness and clear lines of communication about sex, your teenager will stand a much higher chance of being able to do the same.

Never Surrender!

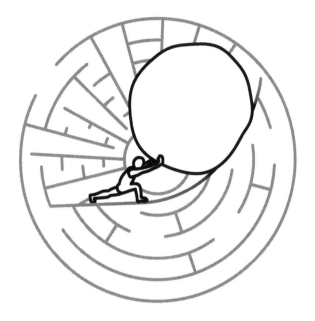

*The struggle itself toward the heights
is enough to fill a man's heart.*
—Albert Camus

I wrote all of the epigraphs for the previous chapters, but this one is from Camus. It is the next to last line of his essay, "The Myth of Sisyphus." Sisyphus was condemned by the gods to roll a boulder up a hill for eternity. At first glance, Sisyphus is in hell. He is set at hopeless, thankless, repetitive work with no rest, forever. This is widely understood as a punishing existence. Albert Camus, though, had a different take on Sisyphus's experience. Rather than focus on the moments when he is set against the stone, pushing, Camus focused on Sisyphus's walk down the hill, following the boulder. It is a space of grace and joy, without struggle.

Conversations about sexuality with your teen may occasionally feel like pushing Sisyphus's boulder. It's true—these may be some hard conversations. But I hope that this chapter—and, indeed, your experiences after putting these rules into practice—will give you a glimpse of the joy that comes from hard work. There are rich, beautiful, relational rewards that come from engaging in really good, deep conversations with your teen.

There may be hard times, places where your relationship with your teenager may feel like you're pushing a big rock up a hill. And now we come to one of the hardest times, one of the biggest reasons parents give for not being able to take my suggestions to heart is when their teenager checks out of the parent-child relationship. She may seclude herself in her room, give one word answers, roll her eyes, and do everything she can to tell you that she doesn't want to engage with you. But you can't let that stop you from continuing the work of being present in that relationship. You must continue to show up. You are her parent, which is a deep connection, and because of that, she cares very deeply about what you think and feel—even if she denies it, to you and to herself. No matter what, it is inside her. If you withdraw from the relationship, too, it will be a much slower process to close the division between you. But if you stay engaged, if you continue to act and believe that the two of you have a relationship, if you always have your hand out in love and openness, your teenager will be able to return to the relationship much more easily.

Doing this is really, really hard. It may be the hardest thing I've asked you to do in this entire book. Continuing to be open to someone who is closed to you can be emotionally draining. In order to support you, here is some acknowledgement of the difficulty and encouragement for continuing that you can read and return to when you're feeling down:

ACKNOWLEDGMENT AND ENCOURAGEMENT

The approach I am suggesting for interacting with your adolescent around issues of sex, sexuality, and romance is not always easy. While I acknowledge these difficulties throughout the book, I want to specifically point out the positive nature of the relational growth you are doing here, as well as encourage you to believe in your ability to push through the difficulties. This applies to every point in this book. I've noted a few places where, if you are struggling, you can come to this chapter. This is the piece I hope you'll read and really take to heart.

Rerouting your conversational patterns with your teenager and opening up the floor to conversations about sex is really, really hard!

What you're doing *is* a challenge, and you *are* up to that challenge. It may take you some time to reach your final goal of solid, smooth parent-teen communication about sexuality, and that's OK. Your understanding of exactly what constitutes solid, smooth parent-teen communication might change during this process, and that's OK, too.

Remember to keep working through the difficulties. Even if you only make it part way to your goal of engaging in conversation with your teenager in the ways I am suggesting, that is OK. You will be doing your best in your time and your place, and you will see positive results in your relationship with your teenager.

Do you have little good-morning and good-night rituals? What do they look like? If you don't, try one for a week and come back and write down how it felt for you.

If you keep at it, it will get easier tomorrow, next week, next month—over time, your communication with your teenager about sexuality will improve dramatically.

You can do this. I promise.

And here are a few tips and hints of ways that may help you stay more consciously open to your teenager, even through the hard times.

1. **Every morning, say good morning and ask how your teenager slept.** This is something of a social nicety that many families do. When we are grumbly or feel emotional distance from a member of our family, these social niceties can fall by the wayside, leading to awkward or angry silences. But checking in verbally every morning is a lovely reminder that someone is there. Even if your teenager just grunts or rolls her eyes, you have successfully made contact and reminded her of your presence in her life. Be sure to do this even if your teenager doesn't rise until noon or later. It is still her "morning," and touching

base and acknowledging the beginning of her day makes an impact. (Be sure that your good morning is genuinely to touch base and wish her well rather than a sarcastic note of her late wake-up time.) If you don't live with your teenager, or you don't see her frequently, try texting or emailing in the mornings.

2. Every evening, say good night and sleep well. Again, more social niceties. But it is these little, constant reminders that keep parents and children linked over the years of living together. It opens up a tiny space, maybe just a moment, when the two of you are connected. If you head to bed much earlier than your teen, say good night if she is home. If she's not home yet, you can leave a note on her bed or taped to her computer screen, somewhere she'll be sure to notice it. And again, if you don't live with your teen, a text or email will serve the same function.

3. Be sure to set aside times each day (like the good-morning and good-night

123

Workbook
Being Approachable

How and when is your teen most likely to approach you with conversation? If that's never happened before, what activities do you think might be most likely to encourage a conversation with your teen?

How can you increase your teen's opportunities to engage with you?

times) when you and your teenager interact, but when there is a moratorium on the hard stuff. Your relationship needs times that are free of questioning, when you just exist together as family. Families find they can fit these times into their schedules in a number of ways. Some families make meal times off-limits for arguments, some families prefer to keep drives or shared television shows or housecleaning or board games as times that are kept apart from arguing or asking difficult questions. Other families find these times to be perfect for these "hard" conversations because it's the time when they are together. And that's fine— as long as there is at least one space or activity where your relationship is always free from those pulls, and you can just have fun together.

4. Always have your eyes, ears, and heart open for a conversation starter from your teenager. Teenagers can leap to conclusions like an Olympic long jumper. They walk into the kitchen wanting to talk, see

you've got your head down in a cookbook, and leave, assuming you didn't want to talk. Teenagers may be especially prone to this kind of assumption about parental noninterest when the topic is something heavy, one that they feel the most shy and awkward talking about—like sex. You are not your teenager, and you cannot make her come and talk to you. But you can stay aware of when she is lurking about, clearing her throat, and looking shifty-eyed at you more often than usual. When this happens, keep doing what you've already started doing, and ask an open, generic question. Hopefully getting talking will help pull her into conversation.

5. Have conversation topics saved up. When you hear of a new book, movie, or song, or when you hear a funny or interesting story that you think might appeal to your teenager, tuck it away on a list in your wallet or your phone. You can also have some you don't know if your teenager would like—she's changing

125

fast, and it can be hard to keep up. Keeping this running list will help you keep your teenager in your thoughts in a positive way, and it will give you a storehouse of choices you can draw on when a conversation about something that isn't negative seems to be needed but is difficult to get started. The best things to bring to the table are funny or intellectually or morally engaging in some way. Be sure and attend to your teenager's answer, and take it as or more seriously than the way she presents it to you.

6. **If your teenage is dating someone, ask after that person.** Not about their relationship, not how their grades are, whether they're going to graduate, or make a lot of money eventually. Just ask about the person, "How's Robin doing?" If you know of an activity or interest of your teenager's love interest, you can ask about that, too: "How have practices been for Robin this season?" Even if you really, really dislike Robin and feel that the relationship is not good for your teenager, asking after her sweetheart will open up space in your relationship with your teenager. And that is far, far more important in the long run than stating (or restating) your negative opinions.

7. **If at first you don't succeed at these steps, be gentle** with yourself. Try and try again.

Now, you certainly don't have to do all of these things. Actually, you could do none of them. It is the act of staying engaged, loving, and present in your teenager's life that matters. If you keep your presence kind, loving, open, and secure, your relationship will either stay strong or will start to rebuild. A strong relationship is the foundation, the bedrock, for supporting your teenager to make the best sexual decisions she can possibly make.

Never surrender and never give up. You are a loving, caring, supportive parent. Your continued presence in your teenager's life makes a difference to her, even if she doesn't know how to show it yet, or maybe doesn't even recognize it.

And here at the last, we return through Sisyphus to Camus. The very last sentence in his essay is this: "One must imagine Sisyphus happy." And I imagine you, set on your path, engaged with your teen, knowing that particular joy of parenting through the hard times and the connection that comes from it.

CHAPTER 11

The Ten Rules

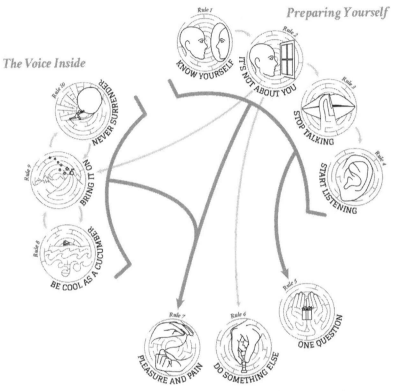

Preparing Yourself

The Voice Inside

Rule 1 KNOW YOURSELF

Rule 2 IT'S NOT ABOUT YOU

Rule 3 STOP TALKING

Rule 4 START LISTENING

Rule 10 NEVER SURRENDER

Rule 9 BRING IT ON

Rule 8 BE COOL AS A CUCUMBER

Rule 7 PLEASURE AND PAIN

Rule 6 DO SOMETHING ELSE

Rule 5 ONE QUESTION

When You & Your Teen Talk

A diagram for understanding

The three sections in this book form a basis for a new, deeper, more meaningful approach to your parent-teen relationship. The rules are sequential, but they are also interrelated. Now that you have an understanding of what each rule and each section are about when taken individually, it's time to connect them. Understanding the relationships between

Preparing Yourself

the rules will allow you to continue to expand on them as you continue engaging with your teen over time.

You'll notice that in the diagram, everything flows from the first section, so we're going to start there. For the time being, just focus on the arrows between the first four rules and not the arrows leading away from them.

There are few things more elemental to effective communication than knowing and understanding your own self. In the context we're talking about in this book, knowing yourself is about knowing your internal feelings about and cognitive models of adolescents, sexuality, romance, and the integration of those three things. Without that bedrock, you'll have a difficult time talking with your teen without unintentional emotional spillover.

Knowing who you are serves as a cognitive flag because when you have an emotional response you will be able to more easily recognize that it may be more about you than it is about your teen. Recognizing those flags for what they are—issues for you to deal with, not issues for your teen—takes you into the next rule. When you are able to recognize issues as your own rather than as something that is your teen's fault or something your teen has to answer to or follow along with, you find the space to pull back verbally.

Your teen has his own stuff. If he's talking with you, he's probably trying to figure that stuff out. Letting him talk (rather than having him listen to you talk) enhances his ability to process. He may be growing up, but you still need to process your emotions elsewhere rather than through or with your teen. Letting go of this outer dialogue allows you to focus on the inner dialogue. The act of listening to your teenager is an internal process of focusing attention on your teen and letting go of your internal dialogue. It requires a clear headspace and intentionality.

These four rules often need to be visited and revisited multiple times over the years, as your teen gets older and brings more complex sexual and romantic topics to the table. As is clear from the diagram, almost everything else you'll be doing with your teen in your conversations about sex and sexuality is based here. Don't feel bad if you end up spending a lot of time in this section. It will prove very powerful as you move into section 2.

I want to jump ahead to section 3, because these last three rules are also mutually supportive of one another and of your ability to take the rules in section 2.

These three rules can be summed up as follows: Stay calm. Be brave. Don't give up. In order to do any one of them, you must be prepared to do all three of them.

- To stay calm in your approach to conversations, you

The Voice Inside

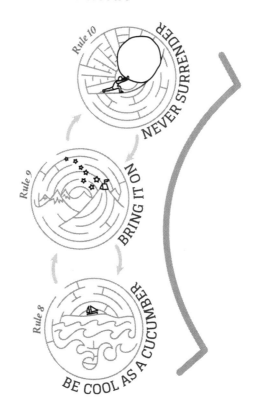

must be both courageous and persistent.

- To be brave, you must be steadfastly dedicated to maintaining your center.
- To keep yourself from giving up, you must have a positive dedication to serenity, both within yourself and in your relationship with your teen.

These are the elements that will keep you on your path, both joyous and trying by turns, toward more fluid, interesting, and educational conversations about sexuality with your teen. These are the encouraging words that you can start to whisper to yourself when you hit a bump that slows you down.

In the full diagram, you'll notice that being able to achieve this section of rules is predicated on rule two: It's not about you. Remembering that the focus of the conversations and your attention should be on your teen rather than on yourself actually allows you to reach these three rules more easily. By taking your own ego out of an emotional situation, you are more fully able to offer up your most collected, most indomitable, most present self. These elements lead directly from the kind of selflessness that arises from recognizing your teen as the focus of the conversation.

The last section of the diagram (and the second section in the rules) gives you guidance to use on the ground, in the moment, with your teen.

You'll notice that unlike the other two sections, these rules are not inherently mutually supportive. They all provide for a higher quality conversation, but they do not need one another in order to be effective. What they do need, however, is all of the other rules.

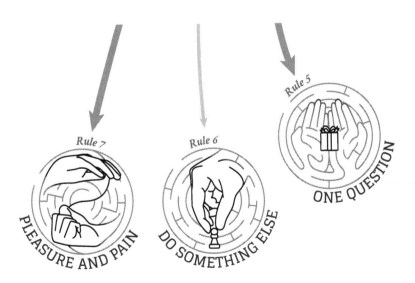

When You & Your Teen Talk

The skill of asking one question—one really good, thoughtful question—is based entirely on the first four rules. Being able to set yourself aside and listen to what your teen needs allows you to discover what to ask, and eventually, after some trial and error, how to ask it.

Knowing whether to do something else during your conversations—and what that thing might be—follows from allowing yourself to be guided by your knowledge of your teen and your acceptance of his conversational needs rather than only looking internally at what would be best for you. This is not to say that you should do whatever it is your teen wants—but rather that when you make the process easier for him, it will allow for more conversations to happen. It is about recognizing that he is discovering sexuality and is still at the very beginning stages of learning how to talk about it. You may be just learning too, but as the adult, you have more options to increase your skill set outside of your conversations with your teen and more reason for doing so. You are the consultant now, no longer the boss. Listening whenever possible to your teen's verbal and nonverbal communication about what he wants and needs will yield far more open conversations.

Rule seven may be the most difficult piece of what I am inviting you to do in this entire book. All arrows point to seven for a good reason. Inviting in the good and the bad in equal measure requires a deep balance of self, a capacity to listen well, and deep reserves of calmness, bravery, and devotion to continuing the conversation. The painful parts about sexual connections are, paradoxically, often the most familiar when we're talking with our teens about sex. But that doesn't make them easy. Even considered theoretically, they trigger and challenge us in our own histories. If they become a reality, they test our reserves and our resources.

While the good things in life are typically easier to talk about than the bad, this is not generally the case with sexuality, particularly as it applies to our teenagers. Holding a realistic conversation with your teenager about good sexual connections is not the kind of conversation that is typically modeled in our culture. Even the small act of saying the words "sexual pleasure" and "orgasm" in conversation with your teenager might feel like an insurmountable challenge. But it is not insurmountable! Drawing on the first section of this book to prepare you and on the third section to keep you going, you have what it takes to have these conversations, too.

The relationships among these ten rules are powerful. They can inform and propel you when the individual rules themselves aren't enough. When you feel some part of your dialogues with your teen failing, come back to this chapter. Spend some time with the diagram. Think about what you can do to bring balance back to the conversation. And remember that just because your teenager is on a roller coaster, you don't have to get on that ride, too. It is better for both you and your teen if you keep your feet on the ground. So if the dialogues aren't going well because your teen is on a roller coaster, let that ride happen. When he's ready to come back to solid ground, you'll be there, waiting with open and loving arms.

CHAPTER 12

Conclusion

I wish I could anticipate every situation, every teen's needs, every parent's insecurities in this book—but I'm only human. I may not have spoken directly to what you need, but I hope that I've given you enough general signposts that you're able to get yourself pointed in the right direction.

I want to end with a few stories. They're things that really happened, although the details have been shifted a little to respect everyone's privacy. All of these parents wanted the best for their teens and were parenting in the way they thought would bring the most value and support to their teens. Their approaches did not quite meet their teens' needs in the best possible way; hopefully, you will spend some time considering how you might be able to do things differently.

PAULA AND MARIE

Paula has a sixteen-year-old daughter named Marie. Paula believes that since her daughter has not mentioned any boyfriends at home and has certainly never brought any around to visit, she has not had a boyfriend yet. Paula set down the rule long ago that Marie could not date until she was sixteen.

When Marie was thirteen, she realized she was interested in dating boys and girls. Around that time, she met a girl she wanted to date. Because of her mother's rule, she did not mention her at home. This relationship, and others with both boys and girls, came and went. Eventually Marie wanted to actually go out with her girlfriend on a real date. She told her mother she was going out with her friend, Sara. Paula did not think there was anything other than a friendly movie going experience and even drove the young couple. Marie and Sara made out heavily in the back of the theater. The relationship ended, as many adolescent relationships do.

About a year ago, Marie met Charlie. Charlie swept Marie off her feet! He was attentive at school and very romantic! He held her hand between classes, he never pressured her to do anything more than kiss, and he brought her flowers on their three-month anniversary. Marie didn't want to throw the anniversary flowers out, but she couldn't hide them from her mother as she had his love letters. So Marie lied to her mother for the first time and said they were from a female friend.

A few months later, Marie told Charlie she loved him, and he said he loved her, too. Making out in the back of movie theaters on double dates had gotten old, so they made a date to meet at Charlie's house when his parents were not there. Marie had gotten used to lying to her mother about Charlie by this point, so it was relatively easy for her to tell her mother she was going to be at the library with a study group that afternoon. Marie and Charlie made this a weekly date. After several more months, Marie and Charlie were engaging in most sexual activity except intercourse. They decided to have sex on their first anniversary, which was coming up soon. Charlie shyly offered to get a condom.

One evening, Paula told Marie that she was looking forward to meeting Marie's first boyfriend soon. Marie laughed. Paula was not sure whether Marie was laughing because she didn't expect to have a boyfriend soon or because she already had one. Paula asked Marie why she was laughing, and Marie brushed her off. Marie and Charlie had intercourse on their anniversary, and it was a loving and connecting experience for both of them.

MIGUEL AND ANNA

Miguel and his girlfriend, Anna, are fourteen and have known each other since they were little. They have been dating for several months. Their parents are close friends. The rules for the couple are the same within both families: Miguel and Anna may not be alone together. There is always a parent present in the house, or the couple may be at the movies or in another public place. The parents are aware that the couple occasionally kisses on the back porch, but they are never in bedrooms or behind closed doors. The parents are not aware how sexually advanced the couple has gotten in these open spaces: Miguel and Anna have started having oral sex. Both Miguel and Anna take turns pleasing each other, and they find it a mutually enjoyable experience.

After some time, Miguel and Anna decide to have sexual intercourse. Miguel obtains a condom, and at the next opportunity, they go to Anna's backyard and have sex. The entire experience takes about ten minutes, and they don't end up using the condom. Neither

Workbook
Paula and Marie

How could this have turned out better for everyone involved? Which section or rule would you suggest Paula think about? Why?

139

Workbook
Miguel and Anna

How could this have turned out better for everyone involved? Which section or what rule would you suggest Anna's mother think about? Why?

of them enjoyed it, and they decide not to do it again. In the coming weeks, Anna is worried that she might be pregnant, so she tells her mother. They go to the store and get a pregnancy test. Anna is not pregnant. However, without talking to Anna, her mother tells Miguel's parents that they had intercourse. Both sets of parents are upset and feel betrayed by their teens. Miguel's parents end their friendship with Anna's parents and want Miguel to break up with Anna because they believe she is a bad influence.

ANTHONY AND JACKSON

Anthony had been very sexual during his teenage and young adult years, sleeping with many men and women. Eventually he met a woman, fell in love, and married her. Monogamy was difficult for him, but he adhered to it because it was important to his wife.

Anthony's son, Jackson, was not as sexual as Anthony had been and was still entirely uninterested in dating. However, Anthony's adolescent experiences had taught him that teenagers had sex starting at young ages (thirteen or fourteen) and then lied to their parents about it. So when Jackson told Anthony that he did not have a girlfriend and was not interested in sex, Anthony thought Jackson was lying in the same way that he had as a teenager.

Anthony felt that sex education was really, really important and so made sex an open and frequent conversational subject. He asked whether Jackson was gay and assured him that was OK, too. Jackson felt increasingly alienated by these conversations about sex and his father's insistence that it was OK for Jackson to be honest about his sexual experiences—when he was already being honest about being uninterested.

Jackson met someone he wanted to be physical with when he was in his early twenties. He would have liked to be able to talk with his father about his new experiences, but he was worried what Anthony would say about him waiting so long.

JULIAN

Julian was fifteen and gay. Or maybe he was bisexual. He wasn't

Workbook
Anthony and Jackson

How could this have turned out better for everyone involved? Which section or what rule would you suggest Anthony think about? Why?

141

Workbook
Julian

How could this have turned out better for everyone involved? Which section or what rule would you suggest Julian's dad think about? Why?

really sure, when it came right down to it. But whatever he was, he was sure his parents didn't think he was anything other than straight. While Julian and his parents knew gay adults and his parents had never seemed bothered by that, Julian still worried about what they would say if they found out he was gay or bi or whatever he was, so he didn't tell them.

One day, Julian's dad got upset because of a selfie Julian had put online. Julian's dad didn't think it was safe to put personal pictures online. Julian was tired from a long day at school when his dad approached him and started lecturing about Internet safety. Julian ended up yelling at his dad, mostly because he was worn out, and telling his dad to stay out of his life and stop following him on social media. His dad yelled back about needing to know what was going on so he could keep him safe. Julian felt attacked and like his dad was trying to run his life—he announced he was gay and then ran to his room and slammed the door.

Julian's dad was stunned—didn't Julian have a girlfriend? It wasn't that he was upset to learn that Julian was gay, but he was still upset about the picture online, and now he felt lied to because he thought Julian had a girlfriend. He went to Julian's room, opened the door, and demanded that Julian explain himself. The situation unraveled from there. Julian shut down and refused to continue the conversation.

Julian's dad really loved his son and wanted to help him work through this potentially trying and emotional time, so he continued to try to question Julian about his sexual orientation over the coming weeks. Julian never opened back up and in fact continued to shut down further. It has been almost two years, and Julian has not talked with his father about anyone he has dated and has not brought anyone home to be introduced to his family. Julian's father suspects that his son continues to date but is unsure how to heal this negative part of their relationship.

I am not going to print my answers to the workbook prompts to these stories because I want you to think deeply about the scenarios and how they might have gone differently. The point of asking you to consider different approaches the parents in these stories could have taken is not that you come to understand the right way or the only way, but rather that you find your way—one that is respectful, open, and honest, among other things.

THE TEN RULES ARE JUST THE START

Take what you've learned here and pull it into your daily interactions and conversations. Focus on your teen as the primary source of interest and storytelling in your parent-teen conversations (remember the conversation between Margaret and her mother in chapter 2). Accept your role as the parent-consultant. It means that your teen is gaining internal strength and independence, which are both necessary for her to lead a happy, fulfilling, loving life. Remember from the introduction that your work as a parent in these conversations is interactive, interdependent, and circular rather than linear.

The ten rules are, in many ways, merely the beginning of what will, hopefully, be a lifelong dialogue. They offer you an initial direction to go in, a framework to use to get started. But the hard work is what you take out of these rules and bring to the actual, real life conversation.

IF THIS IS JUST THE START, WHAT'S NEXT?

It's the real world that's next—the actual starting, engaging in, and continuing conversations with your teen. At least, that's what's next in the relatively narrow realm of your parent-child relationship that is about sex and sexuality. But there is so much more to who you are—to who they are—and to what your relationship can be. I hope you're excited to continue to learn more about all of those things.

On the inevitable days when you feel that this parenting thing isn't easy, remember that regardless of the age of your child, it is also rewarding. When your teens were little, you needed support; now that they're teenagers, you still need support. There were playgroups and parenting classes and support groups and informal moms and dads groups that all sprang up around families with infants, toddlers, and young children. These can dissipate as our children age into adolescence—but we don't need the support any less. Don't be afraid to reach out. We all need community. If you can't find a support group in your area, get one started yourself.

Here are some other things that you and your teen could do together: taking a shared pottery class, planning day trips to all of the small towns within two hours of you, reading a book at the same time and talking about it together, watching all of the Harry Potter movies over a weekend and making up your own spells, buying a new video game and playing it together until you beat it, making s'mores over your gas stove, or planting a tree. But if you can't do any of those things, at least eat dinner together tonight.

And so, in order to bolster and buoy you up during the trying times, here are the epigraphs from each chapter, a little bit different than they were, with extra affirmations, because I believe in you.

The center of a circle is its balance point.
The balance of my relationships is at my center.
I know my center. I can begin.

Discovery is a beautiful thing, and
there is much more to find, learn, and understand!

The other that is mysterious continues to draw me in,
and I am learning to explore gently, kindly, and with compassion.

I listen from the quiet parts in me to the quiet parts in others.

To pause, wait, and consider is to offer
the gift of the space between the stars
so that the brightest one can shine.

Conversation is an act of creation,
and we can create together.

The heights and the depths, they both hold truths, and must be welcomed.

I am as deep as the ocean.
I am as timeless as the stones.
I breathe in and I breathe out.

I embody bravery, inside and out.
I am as unshockable as the stars.
I trust in myself.

The struggle itself toward the heights is enough to fill a man's heart.
—Albert Camus

And if you take nothing else from this book, please take this:

Pay attention.

Stay engaged.

Keep listening.

You can and will make a difference.

You can and will continue to build (or rebuild) a relationship with your teen.

ACKNOWLEDGEMENTS

My Heartfelt Thanks

This book began as a twinkle in my eye many years ago, as I was getting my toes wet as a sex educator. That it is now in physical being, eight years later, is amazing to me. There are many people who have done many things in support of me and Breaking the Hush Factor. Below are a few of them.

First, the people who donated in the first week to my Indiegogo Campaign! That the first few days had such a strong and wonderful response was very meaningful to me. Here are a few of those donors, along with bits and pieces of information about some of them and why they are dear to me and to this book:

- Yoni Alkon
- Kellie Bledsoe
- Theresa Clark
- Thia Coward - You're amazing in so many ways. We should hang out more.
- Joan Garrity
- Brenda Gomez
- Laura Hancock - I am so happy to have you as a colleague! www.DrLauraHancock.com
- Robert L. Heil - I've already thanked you, but you're worth mentioning twice!
- Robert Hill
- Jeanine Johnson
- Valkyrie Lang
- Betsy Neale
- Joleen Nevers
- Marg Pedroza

- Dorian Rinehart - Thank you to my amazing mother, who taught me so much about parental love.
- Ruth Rinehart - Thank you to my wonderful aunt!
- Margie Roesch
- Marygrace S. Sorensen
- Teri C. Sperry - Who does phenomenal work in alternative education in Austin, TX! www.AltEdAustin.com
- Nicole Petta - Your endless enthusiasm and dedication are so powerful.
- Elizabeth Uzelac
- Michael Wilkes

Second, a few more specific people who always deserve my gratitude and thanks:

- Alice Fielding, one of my best friends, who lovingly read, commented, and edited this book multiple times!
- Bill Taverner, my mentor and friend.
- Taylor Martin, my graduate advisor.
- Kevin and Lynda Morgan, my father and stepmother.
- Mosch Virshup, my stepfather.
- Keely Wahl, one of my best friends, who keeps me super real.

I love that it took so many people to make this book a real thing. Thank you, all of you!

Meet Dr. Karen Rayne

Dr. Karen Rayne began her work in education almost two decades ago and her work with parents of teenagers almost ten years ago. Since then she has been working in her local community, as well as nationally and internationally, to support parent-teen conversations about sex and sexuality. She has worked with parents, youth, and professionals on this topic. Her primary goal is to support families in building relationships that hold solid and true from the fun times through the hard times and everything in between. Sexuality is all of these things, and so conversations about them must also be.

Karen is based in Austin, TX, where she consults parents and teens and teaches comprehensive sexuality education, and she blogs at Unhushed.net.